MW01199199

"When Jim told me in the Indianapolis, 'I think God] knew he was serious. He ha a gift of discernment and I could tell that in this moment, Jim was not kidding. His humor wasn't lost on the folks at TCM International Institute when he said, 'April 1, 2013 is the day we will start.' Trust me when I say Jim is no fool. He answered God's call and learned more about our Lord everyday as he leaned into the Father. He shares the spirit of his and Glenda's walk in this wonderful book. I encourage you to sit down, read, and take a walk with Jim and Glenda Buckley."

-David Wright
Vice President of Ministry Services, TCM International

"When Jim first told me that God was leading him to walk across America, I am sure I had the same bewildered look that folks had when Noah said, 'God wants me to build an ark' or when Moses said, 'God spoke to me from a burning bush.' It sounded a bit crazy, but the things God calls us to often seem crazy to us at the time. All I know is that Jim, just like Noah and Moses, was obedient and that has been the hallmark of Jim and Glenda's lives. This book follows a journey of obedience, day by day, mile by mile, step by step… every step, a step of obedience. I believe Jim and Glenda's experience will inspire you to hear God's call, however crazy it may seem, and walk in obedience!"

-Ken LaMont
Lead Pastor, Newbury Park First Christian Church

"As we ate our fish tacos, Jim, acting like an excited seven-year-old telling his friend about his next great adventure, told me he was going to invite individuals to 'come home' as he walked into their homes across America. The joy on Jim's face was compelling. On his return, that joy had increased 100 fold because Jim rediscovered a profound truth in Christ, Jim never walked alone. *Walking Across America* reveals that truth through the many experiences Jim and Glenda had on their adventure. From the very beginning when The Walk lived as an idea in Jim's heart, to the end when his family joined him on the bridge to New York, I have been encouraged to follow in Jim's footsteps – to use every opportunity God gives me through the day to invite others home to Jesus and to abide in God's constant presence throughout my day. As you read *Walking Across America* will you discover that God has never left you as well."

-Tom Stephen
Pastor, Monte Vista Presbyterian Church

"Jim Buckley's obedience to walk across America and call attention to the home, inspires me to obey God's call, even if it seems random and uncomfortable."

-Timothy Smith
Author, Family Coach

"This book is about God inviting a man to go on a walk...a *Walk Across America*. God gave Jim Buckley a passion, rooted in his intimate relationship with Jesus, for people...families, to have Jesus be the center and heart of the home. This passion became the message of hope God wanted him to share with everyone he met. What better way than to walk and talk with people along the byways of America. As you read, you discover his walk is much like life, filled with wonderful surprises, hurdles to overcome, hills, valleys and curves. Along with his wife Glenda as his support, this wonderful book invites you to share their adventure and meet the people God brought into their life as He walked along with them."

-Linda Kirk
Executive Assistant, Newbury Park Christian Church

"*Walking Across America* applies to all of our lives when we personally choose to walk every step with Jesus. The depth as well as the simplicity of Jim and Glenda's commitment and obedience to follow where God leads is not only inspiring, it is life changing. Imagine the impact on each of us, our families, and our country when we never walk alone, knowing that Jesus is with us no matter where He leads...across the the country, across the street, and in our own homes."

-Leslie E Haggard
Director of Inviting America Home & Walk Coordinator

"It was an amazing moment when God spoke to my husband and me and said, 'Turn your car around.' (That was not something either of us would have normally done.) We met Dr. Jim Buckley walking across America. He was a person whose love of God guided us. His conviction and very strength of belief gave strength to believe the miracles we were later given in a time that seemed hopeless. God's blessing was truly in him as he shared with us."

-Barbara Strenfel
Environmental Public Health Specialist, Poplar Bluff, Missouri

"Glenda Buckley redefines 'suitable helpmeet.' Her steadfast spirit, pleasant demeanor, and can-do approach, coupled with Jim's sense of humor and dogged determination were among God's gifts that enabled them to complete the *Walk.*"

-Carleen Morris
Branson, Missouri

"Sun City West Christian Church had the pleasure of having Jim and Glenda Buckley with us when they passed through our town. Jim had walked about four hundred fifty miles and was very tired with sore feet. Just think, he only had about another three thousand miles to go. What's so wonderful was Jim and Glenda were glorifying Jesus with every step Jim took along the way. PRAISE GOD! PRAISE GOD! PRAISE GOD!"

-Jack Bass
Elder, Sun City West Christian Church, Sun City West, Arizona

"John and I are excited that Jim and Glenda are sharing their exciting story with us—a story of a call he received from God. That call was a test of faith and physical endurance that he passed only because of God's grace and the prayers and support of a godly wife. I wish we could see through God's eyes how many lives were touched and changed and will be changed because of the seeds that were planted. A powerful message of hope was delivered that has to start in the home by putting God first. 'Well done, good and faithful servants.' Before Jesus ascended into heaven, His last words were to instruct His followers to be His witnesses in Jerusalem, in Judea, in Samaria, and even to the remotest part of the earth. For us, that means sharing Jesus in our city, our state, the neighboring state, and in the world. This is what Jim and Glenda Buckley have done."

-Pat Bailey
Austin, Texas

"One of the most exciting weekends of our lives was when Jim and Glenda Buckley showed up at Glenview Christian, Glasgow, KY! I will always cherish the moments we spent together in an impromptu interview sharing our love for Christ Jesus. Jim and Glenda are some of the most wonderful Christian people we have ever met! The book is really just a reflection of their daily walk with the Lord."

-Richard A. Martin
Minister, Glenview Christian Church, Glasgow, KY

"A fascinating recount of the remarkable journey by an amazing couple. The stories highlighted that, no matter the circumstances that we may be facing, God is always with us. Thank you, Jim and Glenda, for reminding us how important it is to share the love of Jesus with everyone we meet."

-Evan Masyr
Executive Vice President and Chief Financial Officer
Salem Communications

"When I met the Buckleys at the RV service center, it was the start of two days of watching God bless them and those around them as they set about doing what had to be done for the walk. My wife, Susan, had to fix them a dinner and my son, Dalton, had to meet them, so that's what we did! They were 'camped' at the Walmart so we went down and spent a while talking in the parking lot about their journey then finished our visit with a circle of prayer before we left them to their dinner. It was an honor and a privilege to meet the Buckleys and to be able to help them in their journey! God Bless you two, and keep it up!"

-Gig, Susan and Dalton Edwards
Blue Ridge, VA

"This is a powerful story about a man who listened when God told him to walk; and how he did it. Reading the pages reminded me of sharing *Walking Across America with Jim* and Glenda.

My prayer is that everyone will be as inspired as I was to share the journey, and now, to read the firsthand account of this inspiring trip, and meet the people whose lives were impacted for the Kingdom."

-Elaine McCoy
President, Terramar Graphics, Inc.

WALKING ACROSS AMERICA

One Step At A Time

Naomi,

Walk with Jesus

Jim & Glenda Buckley

Jim and Glenda Buckley

Luke 19:5

EXULON
ELITE

DEDICATION

I have been reminded of your sincere faith, which first lived in your grandmother Lois and in your mother Eunice, and I am persuaded, now lives in you also. (2 Timothy 1:5)

And the things you have heard me say in the presence of many witnesses entrust to reliable men who will be qualified to teach others. (2 Timothy 2:2)

We dedicate this book to our "family roots"–roots of the past and roots of the future.

We each come from a family of faith in Jesus Christ as Lord and have spent our lives passing on that faith to our children and now our grandchildren.

Roots of the Past

Our parents and grandparents were hardworking farmers and ranchers and people who demonstrated their faith in Jesus. (Jim) Tragedy hit my family when my thirty-seven-year-old mom died suddenly of a heart attack when I was ten. My dad married a Sunday school teacher from our church two years later, and my family grew from two children to seven. Our faith carried us through the challenges and changes. Glenda and I cherish all of our "roots of the past," but will focus on that one person who had a major role in helping me become the man that I needed to be to walk across America.

Grandad Bevley (B) Buckley was an elder in his church and a man of physical and spiritual strength. He was blessed with a sense of humor and fun to be around. On his death bed, he told me he wanted me to officiate his funeral, teasingly suggesting we have a trial run so he could hear all the nice things people would say about him. Some might think that's crazy. I didn't, because I knew his sense of humor came from his strength and depth–deep enough to laugh at life. His faith was so solid that it was leading him home to heaven.

In fact, before our *Walk* began, a friend of one of my grandsons heard I was planning to walk across America and said, "Your grandad is crazy." My grandson smiled and said, "I know." I was honored to be put in the same league as my grandad. (See Appendix A for a discussion of "crazy" people of faith in the Bible's hall of faith in Hebrews 11.)

I saw him as a man who never quit. When work was hard, he never quit. When he faced struggles, his faith grew. His ability to laugh at life, never quit, and his strong faith forged a path I admired. I have lived to follow in his footsteps, steps necessary for me to be able to do whatever God called me to do–even walk across America. In week seventeen, I'll add more about my grandad and why he was special.

To all our foregoing roots we say, "Thank you."

To Grandad Buckley, Glenda and I say, "Thank you for showing us how to walk through life."

Roots of the Future

Our second dedication goes to our roots of the future–our children, their spouses, and our grandchildren – people of pioneering faith, perseverance, and a commitment to having Jesus live in our homes.

We have five children, each married to a marvelous spouse. Three boys: Andrew, Jason and Daniel came first. Then twins, Jamye and Jared, blessed us to complete our five. Andrew married Cheryl, Jason married Brigett, Daniel married Charity, Jamye married Robert, and Jared married Stephanie. We have been blessed with each addition to our family. Each one is a person of faith.

We now have fifteen grandchildren, with one more on the way. At the time of the *Walk*, we had thirteen grandchildren. We walked across the George Washington Bridge with our family of twenty-five that included thirteen grandchildren, five children and spouses, and the two of us. We carried with us items reminding us of two of the family already in heaven–a son and a grandson.

We dedicate this book to our family, who lovingly and sacrificially released us to walk, backed with their prayers and love. They voiced their enthusiasm for our obeying God's calling to bring hope to the homes of America, believing Jesus is the source of that hope.

Our family has been raised with Jesus in our home. We are far from perfect, having been challenged with many difficulties. With Jesus in our home, we have hope that has carried us to victory after victory, even in some dark days.⁻

We love our family and dedicate this book to our roots of the future, our children and grandchildren, life-changers of today and tomorrow. They are marching to heaven where they will join their roots of the past and dwell with God forever.

Grounded in roots of the past and future, it's time to walk across America, one step at a time. Let's go!

-Jim and Glenda Buckley,

Walking through life together;

Walking across America in 2013.

Table of Contents

Pastor Jim Buckley - Walks Across America - April - Oct. 2013

Newbury Park
First Christian
Church

Times Square
New York City

www.InvitingAmericaHome.org

ACKNOWLEDGMENTS

Walking across America is no small task—especially for a man in his upper 60s. It took a lot of prayer and preparation. We are going to acknowledge and thank many people by name who took part in this adventure. For anyone we missed, please add your name to your copy of the book, and we will autograph it to verify that you're part of the team.

Thank you to our editor, Dr. Larry Keefauver, who guided these two "non-authors." He taught us so much while being very warm and patient with us. His own faith was encouraging to us.

Pre-*Walk* People: Thank you to each of the following people who made the adventure so special, even before we started: Pastors Tom Stephen and Tim Smith, encouragers and guides; Jack and Donna Lucas and Steve Covert, early collaborators; Karla Stevenson, videographer; Jason Buckley, RV driver's training; Rick Shima, CPR & First Aid instruction; Mark Johnson, emergency and safety; Lura Biffar, made a *Walk* quilt to be signed along the *Walk*; Jim Martin, manager of Road Runner Sports; Dr. Keith Roberson, Dr. Edward Hanzelik, health advice; Tom Maronde, RV purchase advice; and Eric Ellis, a walk-tracking system. Thank you to all these priceless people who helped even before we left for the *Walk*.

The *Walk* Team: Thank you to each of the very busy members of the *Walk* Team who worked with us all across the 3,131 miles of the *Walk*: Leslie Haggard, *Walk* director of Inviting America Home and *Walk* coordinator, website manager and financial advisor; Jared Buckley, media contact, social media director managing Facebook; Andrew Buckley, safety director, monitoring the *Walk*; Elaine McCoy, printer and advisor; Kecia Davis, trainer, injury and health advisor; and Paula Haydter, who contacted churches and individuals. This amazing team walked with us across America.

Ministers along the *Walk*: Many ministers opened churches, homes, and hearts for us on the *Walk* and they include: Glenn Kirby, Myron Wells, Wayne Dykstra, Larry Hamblen, Jon Forrest, Matthew McCurley, Richie DeMent, Rod Vannoy, Damian Phillips, Terry White, Richard Martin, Shane Nickell, Barry Bryson, Bob Kolodner, Ed Wilson, Ben Cachiaras, and Gary Johnson,

Hospitality People: Some people opened their homes, housing us for a night or more and they include: Rick and Toni Johnson, Jeff and Carleen Morris, Don and Donna Shiflet, Kevin and Sherry McSweeney, with Johnsons and McSweeneys also shuttling us to and from airports. Randy and Rita Thompson opened their storm shelter during a storm in Higgins, Texas.

Special Thanks to: Lead Pastor Ken LaMont and Mark Bodenhamer, elder chairman, for their leadership to keep contact with us and our home church of Newbury Park First Christian Church in the six-month *Walk* and for both being in New York City to celebrate the end of the *Walk*; Billy Graham Evangelistic Association Video Team led by Kevin Adamson with others helping on the five different times the BGEA Team videoed the *Walk*, teaming up with the BGEA to bring hope to the homes of America through Jesus Christ our Lord; David Wright, friend and encourager of the *Walk* and Jim's overseer of his ministry with TCM in Europe, Central Asia, and America; David and Jared produced a keepsake video of *Walk* slides with Johnny Cash singing, "I've Been Everywhere Man."

Thank You to Walkers who walked with Jim: Eric Ellis in California; Pastor Ken LaMont in California and Washington, D.C.; Curtis James in Phoenix; group of six in Phoenix; Rick Rose in Arizona; Jared Buckley in

Arizona and Washington, D.C.; Jon Forrest in New Mexico; Rick Johnson in Texas; Atkinson/Emmons family of five in Virginia; Allen and Gina Blaxton in Virginia and Edgard Mello in Missouri, the only person to walk an entire 25 miles with Jim in one day.

Thank You to All the People we met along the way and especially to those who gave permission to include their names in this book–they are real people!

A Very Special Thank You goes to Linda Kirk who transcribed over 200 pages from the mini-recorder Jim carried daily on the *Walk*. This has become an awesome resource of information (some gibberish) from the actual roads of America.

Thank You to the "Inviting America Home" prayer team. They were so faithful and supportive as Glenda would send updates and prayer requests out to them throughout the *Walk*. What an encouragement it was to know they were "out there" holding us up in prayer.

A Huge and Humble Thank You to our loving and mighty Lord God–Father, Son, and Holy Spirit–Who called us to walk. He protected us, provided for us, delighted us, and was with us every step of the way across America! It was His *Walk*.

Never Once
Matt Redman

Standing on this mountaintop
Looking just how far we've come
Knowing that for every step
You were with us

Kneeling on this battle ground
Seeing just how much You've done
Knowing every victory
Was Your power in us

Scars and struggles on the way
But with joy our hearts can say
Yes, our hearts can say

Never once did we ever walk alone
Never once did You leave us on our own
You are faithful, God, You are faithful

Scars and struggles on the way
But with joy our hearts can say
Never once did we ever walk alone

Carried by Your constant grace
Held within Your perfect peace
Never once, no, we never walk alone

Never once did we ever walk alone
Never once did You leave us on our own
You are faithful, God, You are faithful

Every step we are breathing in Your grace
Evermore we'll be breathing out Your praise
You are faithful, God, You are faithful
You are faithful, God, You are faithful

Songwriters: Jason Ingram, Matt Redman, Tim Wanstall
Published by: Lyrics © Capitol CMG Publishing, LLC,
Sony/ATV Music Publishing LLC, BMG RIGHTS MANAGEMENT US, LLC
Used with permission.

You can visit www.invitingAmericahome.org for more about the story of the Walk and the ministry of Inviting America Home. You can contact us through the website. Included on the website are the pictures from the book in color. Also, there are many more pictures from the Walk on Inviting America Home Facebook. We would love to have you like us on FB.

Jim and Glenda Buckley

****

"Here I am! I stand at the door and knock.
If anyone hears my voice and opens the door,
I will come in and eat with him, and he with me."
(Revelation 3:20)

Preface

Why?

In the beginning, there was one question. Why? Why would anyone walk across America at age sixty-six? Is he crazy?

The "idea" came as a "pop up" in my mind. It was a "pop up" like on a computer. It came out of nowhere. My "pop up" came after an eight-mile early morning walk in Utah, on July 6, 2010, during a visit to one of our sons and his family.

A flash thought crossed my mind, "Why don't you take a long walk?"

Stunned, since I was just finishing a long walk, I responded by thinking, "What should I do? Walk across Utah?"

It was meant as kind of a joke.

I was satisfied with my response until another thought flashed across my mind, "No! Walk across America."

The thought of walking across America had never even crossed my mind. Could this be the Lord "playing with me" or was I losing my mind? Wanting to hear more, I began asking God in a prayerful way some questions, but there were no more flash thoughts except, "Go home."

Interpreting that to mean I should go back to my son's house where my wife, Glenda, and I were staying, I looked at my watch and realized it was about breakfast time, and she would be up. As I headed back, I thought of how I would share these "thoughts" with her and expected her to tell me to go back to bed.

"I think God wants me to walk across America," I said the minute I walked into the house.

She quickly and enthusiastically asked, "Can I go?"

That was not at all what I expected! In fact I was shocked! That "pop up" became an obsession that gave birth to tons of questions!

What is the purpose of this walk?
How do I get ready to walk?
Am I crazy?
How long would the walk take?
How many miles a day would I walk?
Where would I start and end the walk?
Where would I sleep and eat?
At sixty-six, do I have the physical health to make this walk?
What kind of conditioning program would get me ready for such an adventure?
What time of the year would I walk?
How would I finance the walk?

My mind was spinning! The questions kept coming. How would I actually make it walking all the way across America? Maybe the same way we had made it through over forty years of life together: with our faith and the convictions that spring from our faith. We would carry those convictions across America or maybe those convictions would carry us.

Some of those convictions will surface in the stories of the *Walk*. Look for them and know these come from the roots of our faith, which as Christians, are in Jesus Christ as Lord. You'll find these following convictions in various places across America:

Never once did we ever walk alone. How true! Although the title of a song by Matt Redman, it's also the story of the *Walk* across America and the walk of life. Jesus was and has always been with us. He certainly was on the *Walk*. Two men walked with Jesus after the resurrection and commented later, "Were not our hearts burning within us as he talked with us on the road...?" (Luke 24:32).

Our family goal is to get our family to heaven, illustrated at the conclusion of the *Walk* by our family walking together across the bridge from New Jersey to New York. We like what Joshua, the great leader of God's people, said, "...as for me and my household, we will serve the Lord" (Joshua 24:15).

Simple obedience is highly underrated. Some people falsely think you need big obedience for big results. God said "walk." I did. It was simple: one step at a time with huge blessings. Glenda was called to be with me as I walked all the way to New York City in obedience to God to lovingly submit to and cooperate with me. She was amazing! As the Bible says, "...his command is that you walk in love" (2 John 1:6).

The home is the place where Jesus must live to build lives, marriages, and families to impact His world. Glenda and I cherish our home because our hearts are there. We do not have a perfect home or family, yet with Jesus living in our home, He has made the difference, taking a variety of struggles and challenges common to so many homes, and turning adversity into His victory. Jesus understood the value of the home when He said to Zaccheus, "I must stay at your house today" (Luke 19:5).

God's timing is perfect since He *is* in charge. We trust that even though God allows things in life that bring difficulties, He uses the adversity to deepen our lives if we walk with Him. The *Walk* belonged to Jesus. He called. He led. He provided. He worked things out for Glenda and me. We saw the hand of God all over the *Walk* as we had already seen His hand at work in our lives. He is in charge. God said in Jeremiah 29:11, *"For I know the plans I have for you,"* *declares the Lord,* "*plans to prosper you and not to harm you, plans to give you hope and a future.*"

As I dwelt on these convictions coming from our faith, I was beginning to be at peace with all the unanswered questions. The Lord wanted Glenda and me to touch hearts and homes with our lives and our faith, not pushing it on people, but simply "Inviting America Home." I was ready to go!

After thirty-two months of thinking, praying and preparing, the *Walk* began in Newbury Park, California, on April 1, 2013, and ended 3,131 miles and 187 days later in New York City Times Square. The answers to the above questions and the stories of the *Walk* are told as a collection of short stories in a week-by-week fashion. It became a *Walk* that touched a lot of lives, bringing hope to families across America. It touched and changed my wife and me, and we will never be the same.

Dr. Jim Buckley, the man who walked across America and Glenda Buckley, who was with him every step of the way.

Introduction by Jim and Glenda Buckley

Finishing the Walk

G lenda: October 4, 2013, what a morning! There was so much excitement in the hotel even while there were issues to clear up before we proceeded to the George Washington Bridge. There were orange shirts all around with:

MY DAD WALKED ACROSS AMERICA
MY GRANDAD WALKED ACROSS AMERICA
MY HUSBAND WALKED ACROSS AMERICA
I WALKED ACROSS AMERICA

Some friends had already gone on into New York City and would meet us after our crossing the bridge. They would be wearing orange shirts that said, "GOD SAID GO...HE WENT." Only members of our family were still at the hotel ready to leave.

We met in the lobby, then loaded into taxis that would take us to the foot of the bridge where Jim had left off on his *Walk*. We had waited to cross the bridge until all the family came in—all twenty-five of us. We had so many arrangements to take care of, but it all finally came together. What an experience. We were excited that our whole family would be finishing the *Walk* with us.

You see, family is and always has been very important to us. We cleared that up on our first walk together. Jim and I first walked together on October 23, 1965. We walked across the University of Oregon campus to get an ice cream cone. It was the beginning of our dating. Walking was very much a part of our first year of dating. It had to be. Jim did not have a car. We walked wherever we went, hand-in-hand, arm-in-arm, sometimes cuddled under an umbrella in the Eugene, Oregon, wet weather where we attended Northwest Christian College. On those walks, we talked often of family because family was so important to us.

Between that first walk on October 23, 1965, and October 4, 2013, are a lot of details and stories.

Our Most Memorable Moment

Jim: One of the most penetrating questions that Glenda and I have had, as we have shared the story of the *Walk*, came to us at the close of a two-hour dinner meeting that was held to prepare us for a speaking engagement.

The host asked, "Jim, what was your most memorable moment on the *Walk*?"

I was speechless. There were so many memorable moments, so I told him I would have to think about it.

My mind was still spinning as Glenda and I headed home. However, it was not long before I could answer that question and when I told her, Glenda concurred. It was an impacting and emotional moment for us and many other people who witnessed it, experienced it or have heard about it. That moment will be engraved on our hearts and minds forever. Ironically, the entire *Walk* built up to that moment.

I could tell you what it was, but instead come walk with us through the 187 days of the *Walk* as we journey week-by-week across America. In some of the weeks, we will include "memorable moments." Occasionally, we will include some thinking about "our most memorable moment," but the ultimate *"Most Memorable Moment"* (will often be referred to as *MMM*) was off limits to me because it would come near the end of the *Walk* to New York City.

The *Walk* would take over six months across 3,131 miles through challenging terrain, various kinds of weather, and traffic issues. During the *Walk*, I had to limit myself to focusing on the current day, taking only one day at a time.

When asked how I was going to get to New York City, I answered using an old saying, "'How do you eat an elephant? One bite at a time.' So, how do I get to New York City? One step at a time."

The challenge of the *Walk* across America was so formidable that I would not allow my vivid imagination to get ahead of me. I had to work hard each day, focused on that day only in order to stay alive, healthy, and make progress.

Once in a while, flashes of thoughts of what could be our *"Most Memorable Moment"* would surface, but I would shut them off to focus on the present. However, as the *Walk* continued and we moved closer and closer to Times Square where we planned to conclude the *Walk*, my heart began to leap and get excited. There were times when I could begin to see pictures of that moment. One day, tears came as I anticipated that moment. I shut off the thoughts because we were not there yet.

A lot of planning and praying would later go into that moment, but at the beginning of the *Walk* even thinking about that moment, our dream seemed impossible. It was a moment way beyond Glenda and me. It would not and could not happen for many reasons. However, it did!

We pray that you will enjoy every step with us as we walk together across America. It is a *Walk* that changed our lives forever, and we hope that "The

Story of the *Walk*" will impact your life as well. Let's go back now to April 1, 2013, when it all began.

> *Now the Lord said to Abram, "Go from your country and your kindred and your father's house to the land I will show you..." So Abram went....* (Genesis 12:1, 4a ESV)

Week 1

April 1-7, 2013 Newbury Park, CA to Cabazon, CA
148.6 Miles

The Long-Awaited *Walk* Begins

The Launch

What an exciting week! It began on Monday, April 1, with people gathering at the Newbury Park First Christian Church for the "launch."

Glenda and I woke up at 4:00 a.m., so excited that "the day" had arrived when the *Walk* would finally begin. We left the house arriving at the church at 5:30 a.m. I was surprised to see so many people. We thought it would be fun if twenty showed up, but there were about ninety, and this was at an early hour and in a pouring rain for Californians (actually a light drizzle).

After many hugs to those gathered, I said, "Pastor Ken, it is 6:00 a.m., let's pray."

Pastor Ken LaMont prayed and as he said "Amen," I looked at my watch and said, "It is 6:02. Let's go!"

Everyone laughed because I had said I wanted to leave at 6:01. I was walking to the Thousand Oaks Mall, about four miles away. I had given permission for anyone to walk with me to the mall, thinking ten people might. I was wrong. Thirty people walked. I was stoked and so were the thirty. I was walking in the lead and pacing myself at a slow walk of about 3.5 mph, but that was hard because we all wanted to walk faster.

We arrived at the mall at 7:30 a.m. Most walked all the way to the mall where the RV and Glenda met us. We formed a circle, prayed and Glenda and I walked on, officially beginning the *Walk* across America. After a short walk, Glenda went back to get the RV and met me at different points that day.

Eric Ellis, a friend who had walked with me in training walks, did walk part of the way that first day. Eric was "setting up" a Google tracking system so I could be tracked daily by family and the *Walk* team. He walked with me through lunch, then walked back home. He said later in an email that he "lost his legs somewhere on the way home." I, too, was tired at the end of my day of twenty-six and a half miles.

Since we were so close to home, Glenda and I went home and slept in our bed each night until day three. We spent Saturday and Sunday night of that first weekend parked at the Dennis and Rosalie LaMont ranch in Hemet. It was a great week, but I looked forward to Week #2 when we would be out of the Los Angeles basin.

"Forrest Gump is here!"

The first week I was losing weight and very hungry. On Friday, April 5, I decided to stop for a snack at a hot dog place.

Jokingly, I said to the young lady at the counter, "I am walking across America and need a hot dog."

She quickly walked to a friend behind the counter and said, "Forrest Gump is here!"

I laughed and ate my hot dog. Life was good and so was the hot dog.

A Bonus and Blessing for Us

The Billy Graham Evangelistic Association's video team, who filmed the launch of the *Walk* as well as the entire day #1, was a blessing in our first week. They also filmed the day before, Easter Sunday at Newbury Park First Christian Church, and filmed us that afternoon as we made preparations for the *Walk*.

The connection with the Billy Graham Evangelistic Association (BGEA) came after a luncheon hosted by Gospel Light Publishing in Ventura that announced "My Hope" campaign. It was to feature Dr. Billy Graham bringing a message of hope to America. Since the *Walk* was to bring hope to the homes of America, I called BGEA, told them what Glenda and I were doing with the *Walk*. I asked if there were materials that the BGEA could send us to distribute to people and churches as I walked.

They sent material, but also had people calling to ask more about the *Walk*. Those calls led to the video team from BGEA coming to film the last preparations of the *Walk*, the launch, and day #1 of the *Walk*. They were a huge blessing as we began the *Walk*.

A Memorable Moment

Richard and Sonia Cuellar and their children were the first people we visited on the *Walk*. I walked to their home in West Hills, California, and Glenda and I had a great visit with this family. On the *Walk*, we prayed for homes to be open to us to share how to have a home with hope.

Glenn Kirby, pastor of the West Hills Christian Church, set up the meeting with Richard and his family. Pastor Glenn said that he had seldom seen a man whose life had changed so dramatically and quickly as did Richard's.

As we visited for about an hour with Richard and Sonia, he told us how he had been a member of the Mexican Mafia and involved with drugs and alcohol. That all changed the moment he asked Jesus to live in his life and home. He stopped using drugs and alcohol and asked Sonia, the woman he loved and the mother of his children, to marry him. She said she thought he was joking. He wasn't. They married and had an atmosphere in their small apartment that we observed was warm and inviting. Their three boys sat quietly on a couch while we talked. Their daughter, the youngest child, walked around some, but was quiet. They were all well-behaved.

We talked about how Jesus can bring hope and change to any home. They agreed. We could see the joy in this home as we gave them a special prayer book that they could use as a guide to help them pray as a family.

We commended them for their children's excellent behavior. Richard and Sonia told their children that if they were quiet, they would take them to dinner. We assured them that Glenda and I had also used "positive reinforcement" plenty of times with our five children. However, from what we observed, we were not sure if Richard and Sonia had the money to take them to dinner.

After a closing prayer, Glenda said to Richard, "Here. I think God wants you to have this."

She handed Richard a fifty dollar bill that I had handed to her as I was leaving the Oaks Mall. A man named Bob, in Newbury Park, had blessed me and handed it to me. It must have been intended for Richard and Sonia.

I had tears and they did, too, after God provided another blessing for them through a man named Bob, and Glenda.

What a day! What a family! It was just the beginning of meeting many people on the *Walk* across America.

Glenda's Glimpses: Not My Nature

When Jim first came home from his "infamous" walk to announce to me that he thought the Lord was telling him to walk across America, I blurted out, "Can I go?"

Now, that is not my nature at all. I am a "let's see" person. Let me think about it, ponder and get back to you on that. The very fact that I said what I said was part of the confirmation that it was from the Lord. I remember the leap in my heart when he said that.

However, the leap landed, and then I pondered. I started thinking about it and had some second thoughts as Jim began making plans. When I realized I would be away from family for six months, I would get sad. We had many grandkids in town and others we could get to. There would be two new babies just before we left.

Our daughter, Jamye, was living in town and would be having her second baby. I was involved with our son's babies, but as mother of a daughter, I had been very involved in helping with their first baby–kind of mother's call for daughters. Jamye and I cried as we said goodbye. Yet, I knew that if God was truly calling Jim, I would not stand in his way and even more, I would support him. This was my call.

Our learning curve was very steep for a while and actually never ended.

First of all, I had to learn how to drive a motorhome. One of our sons, Jason, is a firefighter and having just been promoted to engineer, he had begun to drive a fire engine. He set me up at our home church parking lot and gave me some pointers on how to drive and park an RV, using side mirrors and little tricks. Then he had me practice. That was very helpful, but getting out on the road was a *whole 'nother ballgame.*

Then there was dumping. Once we were well across Los Angeles, we knew it was time to do it. It just so happened good neighbors of ours were visiting their son who lived near where we were going to dump. These friends decided to help me since Jim was not around. That was the beginning of many "happenings" on the *Walk* that were so timely. Thank you, Tom and Karen! Thank you, Jesus.

I had said early on that I knew God would have surprises for us. I later renamed what I called them, but one of the early surprises was in the parking lot of Azusa Pacific—a skunk in the bushes. I tried to get a picture, but it was difficult because I did not want to roll the window down, and I did not want to alarm him. He was beautiful—from a distance!

Little Did We Know What Was Coming!

Week #1 was an awesome beginning of the *Walk*. We experienced enough joy, excitement, routine, people, places, and challenges that were all bathed in prayer, that we somehow felt we were now "experienced." However, little did we know what the Lord had in store for us! It would be overwhelming at times. We would be broken, as well as humbled, by the Lord's powerful working on the *Walk*.

It was "His Walk," after all. He would make His presence known, but not all at once.

14

REFLECTIONS ON WEEK 1

God provided another blessing for this family through Glenda and a man named Bob.

Our learning curve was very steep for a while and actually never ended.

It was "His Walk," after all. God would make His presence known, but not all at once.

We started this Walk believing we were simply being obedient, not expecting how stretching and trying obedience would be as we walked.
We would learn along the Walk that simple obedience is highly underrated.

******

This is love for God: to obey his commands. (1 John 5:3a)

Week 2

April 8-14 – Cabazon, CA to Parker, AZ
152.9 miles

God's Perfect Timing

A Blur

Week two was a blur. We were so busy walking, visiting, and getting used to life on the road, that I only entered two or three lines in two days of my daily journal. We were exhausted at the end of each day!

This week was filled with excitement—a home visit, physical pain from walking, and the unique beauty of the Mojave Desert. We did not see the animals that are out at night, but we had confidence that they were in the desert. Somehow, they live in a place humans do not live, finding enough water to survive. Our awesome Creator made them so they did not need much water.

Walking through the desert, I knew there would be snakes, but fortunately the only ones I saw were dead, having been run over by cars. A few cars passed us and some stopped to ask if we needed help. After thanking them, we told them why we were walking.

By the end of the second week, we were in Parker, Arizona, and making good time. I just had to remind myself that we live in a very big state. California is very long, but also wider than I realized.

Strong, Gusty Winds in Palm Springs

We had a strong wind storm on Monday, April 8, walking to Palm Springs and north to Yucca Valley. Glenda and I were joined by Pastor Ken LaMont, our lead pastor in Newbury Park. It was a fabulous day to have him there.

Pastor Ken with Jim near Palm Springs on a very windy day

I knew the wind was strong because my easy walking pace of 3.2 mph was increased to 3.8 due to a strong wind blowing behind me and pushing me. One of those gusts (about 60 mph) caught the cabin door of the RV as I was opening it to get a drink of water. The wind threw it back, throwing me to the ground. I hit my head on the passenger door and my shoulder hit the front right wheel of the RV. I was stunned, but not injured seriously. Ken jumped out, pushed the door back, and closed it.

I imagined the worst, primarily that repairing the RV would take extra days and money that we did not have to spare.

God is so good and His timing is perfect.

Not only was Ken able to get the door back in place, but after stopping for the night in Yucca Valley, Ken repaired the door. Ken's dad and mom, Dennis and Rosalie, brought us dinner. Dennis also brought some tools. With his dad's help, Ken was able to put enough screws in the door to reinforce it and hold it. The door worked and was good the rest of the trip. I teased them, though, saying the RV now tilted a little to the right with all the extra screws in the door. What a blessing! Thank you, Ken and Dennis. Thank you, Jesus!

Blisters in the Mojave

After three days of walking through the Mojave Desert, my feet were killing me. I had three painful blisters on my left foot. We doctored them trying different solutions to ease the pain. None worked perfectly, but I kept walking. Other than the pain, I actually enjoyed the Mojave Desert.

---

*Walking with the Lord through His beauty
in the desert was special.*

Saturday, April 14, my **journal** stated, *This was one of the hardest days yet, but I glorify the Lord because it is over.* I made it to Vidal Junction with Glenda washing my feet, using ice water provided by a gracious clerk, Crystal, from the convenience store. What a refreshing and a soothing end to twenty-four blistering miles in ninety-degree heat. I made it by praying a lot and pressing on to the goal of Vidal Junction.

I learned that the heat from the asphalt in the desert made my feet swell. To lessen the pain, I used a very small needle provided for us in a First Aid Kit from a paramedic friend, Rick Shima, to remove the fluid. With disinfectant and secure wrapping, my blisters were manageable and healed quickly using Vaseline and corn patches to cushion the foot area. Future blisters never were as bad after the Mojave.

A better alternative – off the pavement

People to People

Week two involved walking through some remote areas. If we would have skipped miles, as some suggested in those areas with less people, we would have missed meeting people like Myron and Donna Wells, a minister and his wife in Yucca Valley.

Climbing a hill entering Yucca Valley}

Glenda had called Myron and visited with him over the phone, asking if he had a family we could visit that evening. Myron was fascinated with the *Walk* and invited us to lunch. We joined him and his wife for a fascinating visit discovering that we knew many of the same people. It is a small world. The lunch gave me a break from walking. I loved that.

While visiting with Myron, he did have a family we could and did visit. During that visit, we heard about their home and family. We then shared with them our hope for every home to have Jesus living in the home. What a marvelous time meeting and sharing life and hopes for the home with Eron and Michelle Malderwin, a son and an uncle.

Best Tostada Salad Ever

On Wednesday, April 10, after walking twenty-five miles into the Mojave, Glenda picked me up and we drove back to Twentynine Palms to spend the night in an RV camp.

I was famished. Once back in the town, we saw a Mexican Restaurant and decided to eat there. Glenda had seen it earlier in the day, and it was a good find.

We went in and ordered a tostada. Waiting for our food "to go" seemed like eternity for me. The waitress brought us some tortilla chips and salsa. Yummy. We ate them, drank water, and waited.

We took the food to the RV camp, eating before we hooked up, even though it meant hooking up in the dark. Those were the best tostada salads of the entire trip. We had others, but nothing ranked as high in my memory.

Sightseeing

We did not often take time to sightsee–too many miles to cover by foot. We were told to see Joshua National Forest.

It was a loop off the path, but it was one of God's surprises of just how beautiful the desert could be.

We tried to capture the rock formations with their red color on film, but it is difficult to do. You have to be there to really see the true colors and majesty. It took some time, but was well worth it.

RV Life – Finding Stops (In the Middle of the Desert)

As RV rookies, finding a place to stop for the night when there was no RV Park for miles was a problem. In the Mojave Desert, we faced heat issues and the challenge of finding an RV park.

In the Los Angeles basin and even in Yucca Valley, RV places or Walmart parking lots provided for us places to stop at night. In the Mojave, there was just desert. Being rookies, we felt uncomfortable and unsafe dry camping by the roadside. One night we drove at least thirty miles to an RV place. That is a one-hour round trip.

We would become more creative as the *Walk* progressed, but for week two, RV life began to be a challenge. Yet, the *Walk* continued.

Glenda's Glimpses: Challenges

Each area had its challenges. It was easier to see Jim in the desert than later when we had hills and corners. I could see him a long ways off in his orange jacket. My pattern was to park, watch him until I could not see him or he was getting too far away. In the desert, I could see him a long ways and could sit in one place until he was an orange dot. Then I would drive forward, pass him, and drive until I was a ways ahead of him and could see him behind me. When I talk about a book for me, I have two possible titles: *Leapfrogging Across America* or *I Drove Across America – A Half a Mile at a Time*.

I met two special people in Vidal Junction. One was the clerk there. She was a wife and mom. Although I did not visit her in her home, I was able to visit her heart and pray with her because of struggles in her home. The other was a bicyclist from California riding to New York. He was not the only bicyclist we met, but he was a young man with a mission for Jesus. We shared a very similar mission.

Cooking was a challenge. If I waited until Jim was finished walking for the day and we were settled, it would be getting late. As hard as we tried, we just could not seem to get to bed early. That was a big problem for me since I require more sleep than Jim. We did take a short nap after lunch, but that was not always enough for me. There were times that Jim would pass me where I was parked and I was not watching very well–I was leaning over against the window sleeping. So sometimes I got two naps a day.

Anyway, there were times that I would cook along the side of the road. I would start cooking, cooking at a tilt, then Jim would get a little too far away or out of sight, so I would have to turn everything off, lodge the pans somewhere on a hot pad, move the RV, then get everything out and continue cooking.

Jim: I thrived on Glenda's excellent cooking in such a difficult setting. Not only was her food delicious, it was highly nutritious which was essential for my overall health as I walked. She was tenacious in making sure I was eating well. That tenacity was a huge factor in helping a sixty-six-year-old man make it across America. Thank you, Glenda!

REFLECTIONS ON WEEK 2

Walking with the Lord through His beauty in the desert was special.

It was a loop off the path, but it was one of God's surprises of just how beautiful the desert could be.

We realized God's timing is perfect. He showed us His amazing timing and provided blessings throughout our Walk like Pastor Ken and his parents, just when we needed them.

****

We also rejoice in our sufferings, because we know that suffering produces perseverance; perseverance, character; and character, hope. And hope does not disappoint us. (Romans 5:3-5a)

Week 3

April 15-21 – Parker, AZ to Sun City West, AZ
138.4 Miles

A Message of Hope

Help for RV Rookies

We met Glenn and Bobbi Olmstead at an RV camp in Bouse, Arizona, on Monday. It had been a long day as I had walked twenty-seven miles. We hooked up at the RV camp which was basically deserted since the "snowbirds" were all leaving Arizona.

Glenn came over to talk with us as we hooked up, asking if we needed help. It was obvious we were rookie RV'ers. He offered some helpful suggestions and visited with us. It was nice to talk with someone who had some knowledge of RV camping.

Later that evening, Glenda and I took some *Walk* materials to his RV and met his wife, Bobbi. We also took a quilt given to us by a dear friend, Lura Biffar, and used for people to sign as we walked across America. We shared about the *Walk,* and they shared about their lives. A widow and widower who married recently, they were full-time RV'ers who were moving from Pennsylvania to South Dakota. They were fascinating Christian people who not only visited with us that night, but then followed us on Facebook all across America.

A friendship that started in a deserted RV park in Bouse, one of the small towns in America, found a special place in our hearts because of people the Lord led us to that night.

Excerpts from Real Life on the Walk!

At times I will be including some **excerpts** from my cassette recorder that I carried with me daily. My recordings were transcribed by a very good friend and former colleague of mine at Newbury Park First Christian Church, Linda Kirk. She served as church secretary for thirteen years and is phenomenal. I hope these recordings will give you some of the actual feel of "walking across America."

It is 4:33 p.m. in the afternoon on Tuesday, April 16, 23.4 miles today. I'm still walking down Highway 72 on the way to 60. I'm less than two miles from 60.

We're on our way to a little town called Hope, and that's the core of our message—there's hope for the home.

That's the core of the Billy Graham message, "Hope for America." This town I am approaching embodies that word. I just had a break. I'm going to walk another four to six miles. Meanwhile, Glenda is doing her great support work. She rubbed my feet for the second time today and it was awesome. It just gives me new life. My feet get tired. I've been told that as we get older the tissue breaks down. We don't have as much fatty tissue as we used to have. Therefore, walking long distances is harder on my feet. Well, I thought that it is a good thing we didn't wait another year or two before the Walk if that's true.

She's in the RV cooking some baked chicken and potatoes, which sounds really good. There is just no traffic out here. A jet just flew over a few minutes ago when I was in the RV, really low, and just went sailing by, exciting. It's just clear as a bell out here. The sky is clear. We're surrounded by a few hills. The desolate desert is not as desolate. It does get some moisture here, so there are some green bushes and a tower up ahead of me. I see the semblances of Hope. I see Hope in my future—yes!

Funny Sign

On April 16, we passed through Hope, Arizona, where we took some great pictures. The funniest picture featured a sign that we saw as we were leaving Hope. It said, "Your Now Beyond Hope." Yes, that is what the sign said. It was not intended to be a funny sign. It was a mistake that was not corrected by the sign maker. Grammarians know that it should read, "You're Now Beyond Hope." Since it doesn't, it was grating on anybody who saw it on our Inviting America Home Facebook and knows English grammar. Glenda and I thought it was hilarious, especially after a long day of walking.

Funny sign

Am I Losing My Mind?

April 17 was not just another twenty-four mile day. I thought I was losing my mind. It would not be the last time I would think that on the *Walk*. Two things broke up the monotony of walking twenty-four miles.

First, as I was walking into traffic heading east, I saw a recumbent bicyclist coming toward me. I said, "Hi," but he passed, not responding to me.

Five minutes later I saw four more bicyclists coming toward me. They stopped and we chatted. Seeing my "I'm Walking Across America" shirt, they knew what I was doing without my telling them.

I asked where they were from and two said, "Agoura."

"Wow!" I said, "I'm from Newbury Park." (Towns about twelve miles apart.)

After that, the other two laughed and said, "We're from Newbury Park."

We laughed and talked about it being a small world.

These friendly bicyclists were heading to San Diego after starting in Tucson and were part of "The Old Kranks" bike club. Since I was about the same age, they made me an honorary member out in the middle of nowhere in Arizona.

The second unique thing that happened was the one that made me question my sanity. Since Glenda had not yet found a place to spend the night, she drove ahead about a mile in front of me. She stopped and phoned to tell me she saw a farmhouse and thought it had an RV park sign. Checking it out, she phoned me again to tell me she saw a man in the yard feeding animals. I told her to be careful and stay on the line while she went to ask the man about parking our RV there that night.

What happened next caused me to wonder if Glenda was losing her mind, but later made me wonder if I might be losing mine. I could hear her talking to a man who spoke broken English, but she was getting excited about seeing farm animals. Being raised on a farm, I thought she must have felt like she was home. Then she got really excited. She said she was seeing goats. Then she started counting them, three, four, five, six big goats, then baby goats, maybe ten, twenty, thirty, or more.

I was worried. Glenda is not the kind of person to lose it. She is always stable, yet she said she was seeing thirty or forty baby goats? Glenda does not use drugs or drink alcohol. *It must be the sun,* I thought. *Maybe I was losing my mind?*

Then she said she saw horses and cows, sounding almost delirious with excitement on the phone. Walking into the farm area, I saw the man. He looked safe. Then I saw my wife. She was not losing her mind. There she was, surrounded by goats, but not thirty or forty. She had miscounted. There were over eighty goats, moving so fast they were hard to count. There were horses and cows, too. God took us back to our roots that day as we both were raised on the farm.

Thank you, Lord, for the priceless ending to a long day.

There was a bonus! The man did have an old RV park for "permanent dwellers," but gave us permission to park for just one night, giving us a safe place to park. We were only a few miles from a town that the man described as dangerous.

After camping with the goat farmhand, I safely walked through that "dangerous" town the next day. Thank you, Jesus.

We were reminded, "Never once did we ever walk alone," the words of a song that became very special to us on the Walk.

Glenda's Glimpses: Leapin' Goats

As I mentioned before, I had anticipated surprises on the *Walk*. God is full of delightful surprises and this was one of them. I was literally surrounded by the goats. To the best of my counting ability, there were over fifty nanny goats. Even harder to count were the little baby goats, the kids. They were about ten days old and were running, bouncing, even jumping in the air, then landing in the completely opposite direction. There were at least thirty-five baby goats. The farmhand showed me how to gently hold them–so cute.

Glenda and goats

*The little settlement lived up to its name,
Gladden. We were!*

The next morning after Jim started walking, I had the opportunity to visit with the farmhand's wife and daughters. We talked about Jesus in the home. She gave me some freshly made cheese to take with me. Bless her, Lord. Bless them.

Severe Ankle Pain!

On Saturday, April 20, my left ankle was hurting so bad by noon that I felt like I could not walk any more. At 11:30 a.m., earlier than my normal time for lunch, Glenda insisted I take a breather, rest my ankle, eat lunch, take a nap, and see how it was after that. Glenda's normal remedy for life has always been "take a nap." Not bad advice either.

After lunch and a nap, I wrapped the left ankle and walked. It hurt, but I walked using a cane that we bought to reach stuff in the RV loft over the cab. The cane helped take pressure off the ankle, and I limped into Sun City West, Arizona, where we would spend the weekend.

I knew something was not right, so we prayed it would get better, not worse. We would see on Monday as we began week four.

A Memorable Moment: Welcoming Committee

It is amazing to me that I can still "feel" what I felt that day as I limped into Sun City West, concluding the *Walk* for week three. Maybe we do not easily forget pain. However, I mostly remember the contrast of pain and joy. There was such joy as I made it to the outskirts of Phoenix by the end of week three!

Our "welcoming committee" was comprised of ten people from the Sun City West Christian Church where we would park our RV on Saturday night. We would share the story of the *Walk* in a Sunday School class, then share the story of our work with the TCM mission in the morning service.

It was Saturday, late afternoon, when we met these seniors who were excited to see us. They were impressed by what we had accomplished on the *Walk* so far. That encouraged us and added even more joy to our sense of accomplishment. We ate dinner at *The Hole in One* restaurant, so named because there were so many golf courses around this area. Sitting there in the restaurant, eating delicious meat loaf, resting my tired feet, feeling almost no pain, and just listening to the talk at the table felt so good.

Thinking back to some of my earliest *Walk* preparation days on the farm, I learned to press on in the heat of the day driving the harvester during the summer. There were long, hot days on the farm, but I learned that if I just pressed on, Saturday night would come. Another week would be over, and I could rest on Sunday. That was the feeling I had that night. Proud of what we had accomplished, I loved it all—these people, the food, talking, sharing the story of the *Walk,* and just laughing and visiting. Glenda was obviously having fun as well.

Week four was coming, and we were sure it would be an unforgettable week, but for now, we just celebrated.

We were learning how important it is to celebrate along the Walk.

Never Too Much Praise! We Cherished Every Word!

What carried us across America and kept us going when the going got tough? The Lord Jesus used the praise and encouragement of people that we met along the way to keep us going! Sunday, April 22, we received much praise and encouragement from the wonderful people at the Sun City West Christian Church.

First, Glenda and I shared the story of the *Walk* in adult Sunday School class. The first minister of the church, eighty-two, who was in the class, said to me after the class, "That was really, really, really, really good." The associate minister thought that our presentation of the *Walk* was so good that the whole church should hear it.

Second, I spoke for a few minutes in the morning service as had been previously arranged by the pastor, Wayne Dykstra and his wife, Pat, before we had arrived. (Both were alums with Glenda and me of Northwest Christian College in Eugene, Oregon.) In the service I shared some more about the *Walk,* but primarily spoke about TCM International Institute in Austria where I am an adjunct professor.

It was another great morning. We loved the morning, especially hearing their encouraging words, as well as words from a retired sheriff we met earlier at an RV camp in Wickenburg, Arizona. He shook my hand firmly when he heard what we were doing and why. He looked straight into my eyes and said with tears in his eyes, walking across the nation with a message of hope for the home was desperately needed by our nation.

Cherishing those words would help carry us through week four. It would be one of the toughest of the twenty-seven weeks of the *Walk.*

Before we left the Sun City West Church, Glenda spent some time with a mother of a troubled family, giving her encouragement and hope. Glenda was a dispenser of hope and this mother cherished every word from Glenda. I could see the mom's face light up as she listened to Glenda fill her with hope.

Jack Bass, one of the leaders of the church, gave us warm hugs as we were leaving that morning, encouraging us as we left. He backed up his hugs by praying for us all across America as one who received Glenda's prayer updates.

REFLECTIONS ON WEEK 3

We were on our way to Hope, and that was the core of our message—there is hope for the home.

The little settlement lived up to its name, Gladden. We were, too!

We were learning how important it was to celebrate along the Walk.

Give words of encouragement and hope to someone today. It might just be the "lift" they need to keep going on their "walk" through life.

****

Therefore encourage one another and build each other up, just as in fact you are doing. (1 Thessalonians 5:11)

Week 4

April 22-28 – Sun City West, AZ to Payson, AZ
85 Miles

Turning Point of the *Walk*

Friends from Home

Week four was definitely the shortest distance walked in miles of any of the previous weeks. However, it was the "greatest distance" because of what those miles represented.

It was a humbling, but exciting week. It was a week I felt the prayer support of hundreds of people like never before. What Glenda and I experienced in week four was awesome. We went from brokenness to hope. I met intense pain, but strong determination and intense drive surfaced and won. It was a week that changed everything!

It became the "turning point of the Walk."

The week started as our friends, Curtis and Catherine (Cat) James, from Newbury Park, arrived in Phoenix on Monday, April 22. Curtis walked with me about six miles on the streets of Phoenix while Cat joined Glenda doing some needed shopping. That night they joined us in the home of Curtis' brother as we visited, ate, and blessed their home.

As I walked out of Phoenix the next morning, Curtis and Cat presented us with a special gift before they left to go back to Newbury Park. What a gift it was—ribs and tri-tip! Awesome! Glenda and I hugged them, thanking them for everything! We ate well that night and the next few days, praising God for these very special friends.

Kids Made Me Cry

On Wednesday, April 24, the twenty-fourth day of the *Walk*, I stopped walking earlier than usual (5:10 p.m.) to Skype the LIFT Kids, our church's Wednesday night kid's ministry with whom I had been working for two years. I loved the kids. With the inspiration of their leader, Crystal Stenner, they had decided to have a jog-a-thon to raise money to help with the cost of my thirteen pairs of shoes and three pairs of professional inserts I alternated in the shoes.

The shoes I chose to wear to help my feet the most were top of the line Brooks Glycerin 10s that I purchased through Road Runner Sports in Newbury Park, where the store manager, Jim Martin, and his team, helped me find the right shoes. They were not cheap.

There were seventy kids running or walking, so I figured they might raise a few hundred dollars to help defray some of the cost. That would be a big help. We made the Skype connection and saw family, friends, and the kids that were ready to jog and walk. We prayed.

After the jog-a-thon, they called and reported that the kids had raised $3,000. I cried, overwhelmed by what the kids had done. The cost of the shoes and inserts for the *Walk* was covered completely. What an awesome and touching gift of love from kids, their families, and our leaders. Needless to say, that "made our day." Oh, Lord, thank you!

Ouch and Ouch!

The obstacles we faced in week four were also related to my feet. Most of the entries I recorded that week on my little cassette recorder mentioned my feet. Here is an entry (**excerpt from the road**) that tells the story.

It is Thursday morning, April 25. It is now 8:11. Glenda and I were up at 4:55. We packed up, loaded up, and left the RV camp before 6:00.

After reaching almost 2,700 feet, we are going down a 6 percent grade into a valley, and then we will ascend again. This is going to be an up and down day. My left leg is actually better today, but still hurts. Every step is painful, but manageable. The pain (using a 0 to 10 chart) has been up to seven and eight at times. Yesterday, it diminished to five through the day. Today, it is probably at a four. It hurts, but I am still walking. Thank you, Lord.

I Sat on the Rail with My Head in My Hands

That same day was one of those moments that will stay etched in my memory bank as unforgettable. After walking up and down hills, going from 1,117 to 4,900 feet with an ankle that would not flex, I wrote in my **journal**, *It was really kind of pretty today with rock formations and Joshua trees and mountains and valleys.* I guess I still saw the beauty in the midst of the pain.

After looking forward to the next town, Sunflower, Arizona, I was disappointed that it was not a town. It was a name that turned out to be a private tow-truck business. Sometimes a small town served as a fun stop along the road, but there was no stopping here as the business was all fenced in.

My daily **journal** for that day says: *Long hard day at the "office." Oh my aching left foot/ankle/shin. Wasn't sure what it was until I unwrapped it and iced it tonight. It's the ankle –swollen and won't flex all the way – makes* *walking up and down hills very tough. I even stopped early tonight at 4:30 p.m. Done! At least my left ankle was done.*

It was interesting that I recorded nothing about being "done" on my recorder or the episode that happened next. It was probably that I was hurting so much and so discouraged.

Ankle check

As I walked across a long bridge, I remember feeling the pain, frustration, and exhaustion. When I got to the other side of the bridge, I stopped. Not knowing what to do, I just sat down on the rail of the bridge, put my head in my hands, and said to myself, "I am done!" I did not cry. Truthfully, I did not even know what "done" meant. Was I done for the day or done for the *Walk*? All I knew was at that moment I could walk no more. I called Glenda and asked her to come and pick me up.

Glenda had been told about a mesa, so she drove there and carefully parked so we could exit quickly if needed. We spent a wonderful night on the mesa, alone with Jesus and a few of God's critters. It was a dark, quiet, beautiful moonlit night.

It seemed to be a special gift provided to us after a horrendous day. Thank you, Lord, for being our Provider.

Glenda's Glimpses: Beautiful but Lonely

After scouring the iPad map looking for a place to stay, there were signs telling of this coming "community." By then we had traditional maps and an Arizona Atlas which showed even the names of ranches, but I did not see anything except this one place. When I finally drove up to it, there was just a tow truck company sign, a house, and a shed behind a very securely locked gate. My heart sank. Where were we going to go for the night?

Noticing a phone number for the tow truck, I called and asked if he knew of any place where we could safely park the RV for the night, actually hoping he would invite us to stay there like the goat farmhand. Instead, he directed us to take a road off the highway, Spring Road, and told us to drive a ways until we found a place to park.

We found a mesa that had a beautiful panoramic view. There were signs that someone had camped there before, but not recently. I had mixed emotions about camping there when I saw the skeletons of a few small animals and saw how isolated we were. It had such a beautiful view, no one was around to bother us, and it was quiet, but maybe just a little too quiet. Who would hear us if we needed help? We were not even getting any phone reception.

As we went to bed, we could hear animals out there, but even though the moon was bright, we never saw any. There was one truck that drove by on an old road a few hundred feet away, but we did not see any people for over eight hours.

Excerpt (from cassette recorder) from the Morning After

It is Friday, April 26. I am going downhill from a peak of 4,560 feet at a seven percent down slope. The leg pain seems to be the residual pain from the seriousness of the injury to my left ankle, so I iced it last night which helped. Glenda massaged it and I also put a muscle stimulator on the ankle. I put on tiger balm and went to bed. This morning it was better. The swelling was down some, so I took some ibuprofen, iced it again, and wrapped it in an Ace bandage.

I am walking at 2.8 mph, going downhill. State police came and scolded Glenda saying she could not park against the rail. There is a lot of rail here, so she is going to have trouble parking. It is like a refurbished road with brand new rails.

Glenda was only trying to help me by shielding me from some traffic, knowing it was difficult for me to walk. However, for her safety, the officer was right. Gruff, but right. Glenda needed to be safe. I would be okay.

Glenda's Glimpses: Scolded

Bang, bang, bang on the side of the RV. A gruff voice called out to me. My hand went to the spray I kept handy. I had rehearsed in my head what to do. Our oldest son, Andrew, had worked helping prepare us for various emergencies. One of the things we each had was a small can of pepper spray. We opted not to carry any kind of weapon. When Andrew asked me if I could shoot anybody, I said, "No," so he said that it would not be a good idea. Trouble was, now that I was faced with a potential threat, I realized I did not know how to use the pepper spray. I had never tried it out, but I did have it in hand.

When the face of the gruff voice appeared on the passenger side, it was an Arizona state patrolman. He told me I had to move the rig. I explained to him that the man in the orange jacket ahead was walking across America. Usually, Jim walked into traffic, but because the two opposite-bound lanes were so far apart, he opted to walk with traffic so I could stay with him. With these big curves and cars whizzing by, I could envision a car swinging too wide and hitting Jim, so I decided to stay quite close so that if there was anyone getting hit, it would be me. My reasoning was that I was bigger; so, I explained to the officer that I was protecting Jim.

He continued to scold me saying, "There have been many accidents here and you are not safe. He [Jim] is, you are not. Move the rig."

I did and we were indeed both safe.

The Walk Parallels Life

Life goes on even after a tough and painful day and so did the *Walk*. I hit "the wall," but kept going. That would become the story of the *Walk*. We would face more "walls," but nothing would stop us on the *Walk* across America. Here is an **excerpt** comparing the *Walk* with the Christian life.

This Walk is just loaded with parallels of the Christian life. There are times in our lives when the walk with Jesus gets really hard and long. This Walk is teaching me, as painful as it may be, that we just keep moving.

This is not always a glorious Walk. It is not always fun and games in the Christian life, either. Sometimes, it is drudgery. Sometimes, we just press on. There are times we have to stop, get refreshed, and healed to go on. It is a long walk and the road gets more narrow as we walk. We have peaks and valleys, like

I am having today. We are going up a peak again. Peaks are sometimes harder to climb than you realize. You think peaks would be the glorious part. Well, yeah, when you get there, but you have to climb to get there. A lot of Christians stop short of the peak. The climb is so hard they quit along the way. They wonder why they never had any glory moments in their life. They did not keep going. One foot in front of the other. One step at a time.

How do you get to New York City? The same way you eat an elephant. One bite at a time. How do you walk with Jesus all the days of your life? One foot at a time, one step at a time, and one day at a time. One!

We like to think in terms of thousands in America. We have got to change that. That is why we are saying "go home" to every home. One home at a time. Maybe the Walk is establishing a platform that the world can see.

By walking to lift up the value of every home and the need to give hope to every home, we go back to lifting up the value of one – one home, one life.

I am walking one step at a time to lift up the value of one home. It is not easy, but if I can walk across America one step at a time, then we can reach one home at a time if we do not stop, but just keep reaching.

It may not be easy, but walking across America isn't either. Walking with Jesus every day isn't either, but it is worth it. So, just like I am doing today, keep going. Do not stop. Do not give up. The end (heaven) will be worth it. When troubles come, keep walking. Never give up. With Jesus walking with you, you never walk alone. It is the story of victory, the Christian life, and can be the victory story for your home.

Keep walking like I am, even amidst pain and exhaustion. I am going somewhere and I pray you are, too, all the way to heaven. Having Jesus in your life and home will take you there.

So, we are on to New York, one step at a time! Nothing spectacular. Just one foot in front of the other, daily, just like life.

One Phone Call Changed Everything—April 26-27

On Friday, April 26, we arrived in Payson, Arizona, early as I did not walk a few of the miles because the road having no shoulder was "deemed unsafe" by Glenda. We camped at an RV site which would be home for three nights while "everything changed" for me. The change came as we contemplated what to do for my ailing left ankle.

Saturday morning, I called a friend. Not just any friend, but Kecia Davis, a close friend who has been an athletic trainer for many years at California Lutheran University, as well as a trainer for Newbury Park High School football. In addition, she has worked closely with some of the best orthopedic surgeons in our area.

Miraculously catching her as she was hurriedly leaving for work, I talked fast, explaining my aches and pains. She listened, advised, and gave me hope! She concurred that I should not walk on Saturday or Sunday, ice both feet, take an over-the-counter anti-inflammatory to get the swelling down, rest, and relax. She advised me to start using an Ace elastic brace on both ankles every day, explaining what I was doing was harder on my ankles than anything her athletes do to their ankles. Being diplomatic, she did not say I was old. She just said that her athletes were a lot younger. She is a very good and kind friend.

She added one more thing that changed the *Walk* for the better. She instructed Glenda to massage my feet and ankles on a daily basis for the rest of the *Walk*. Glenda was also instructed to push the poisons up the leg and out of the stressed area. Glenda did that and it was amazing.

I teased Kecia saying, "You are pushing the poisons toward my heart, trying to kill me."

She laughed and said, "No, it will help heal you, not kill you."

By Saturday night, my left leg was better. By Sunday night, it was much better. By Monday morning, I walked without pain. Hallelujah! Thank you, Jesus. Thank you, Kecia. Thank you, Glenda.

Glenda was amazing! From that weekend on to New York, Glenda massaged my feet at noon and at night every single day. She redefined submission, never complaining about massaging my feet. What a woman! If you have not already picked up how amazing Glenda is, stay tuned. You will hear more because she was and is amazing! I could not have made the *Walk* without her. Massaging my feet was only one of the many things she willingly and lovingly did every single day, but it might have been the best. I love Glenda and so do my feet!

That was a phone call that changed everything. Instructions and hope came from Kecia. Hope was becoming the word for the Walk! It was hope that would carry us on all the way to New York City.

Glenda's Glimpses: Not Always Fun

So, this is what "Can I go?" got me into. Rubbing feet is not my idea of fun, but for some reason I did not mind it. Maybe it was because I could physically see the swelling going down as I pushed upward. Maybe it was God's grace. Now, I will not say I never minded it. There were times when

I was so tired that I could barely stand, and I wanted to go to sleep so badly. We were accustomed to praying on our knees every night, but it was difficult to do in the RV so we would pray in bed. Sometimes, Jim would have me pray first because he knew I would be asleep before it was my turn. I was known to fall asleep mid-word in my own prayer. There were many times I would ask in the morning, "Did I pray last night?" and he would just smile.

Now, about submission, I have a comment. Some of you have an issue with that word, but the best of the best knew it well–Jesus. If He could submit, I figured I could, too. Once in a while, I submitted more in action than attitude and I am sorry for that, but I read once that really the word submit means to cooperate and not do battle. Cooperating with your husband is a very good description of submission. In Ephesians 5, the husband is asked to do something so much harder—die for his wife. That can mean a lot of things like die to pride, to selfishness, etc. To me, submit or cooperate is not nearly as difficult, especially because I have a husband who has the heart of Jesus. *Therefore, as I cooperate with Jim, I am cooperating with God.*

REFLECTIONS ON WEEK 4

It seemed to be a special gift provided to us after a horrendous day. Thank you, Lord, for being our Provider.

By walking to lift up the value of every home and the need to give hope to every home, we go back to lifting up the value of one – one home, one life. Hope was becoming the word for the Walk! It was hope that would carry us all the way to New York City.

It may not be easy, but walking across America isn't either.

Walking with Jesus every day is worth it. It is just like I had to do every day, keep going. Do not stop. Do not give up. The end (heaven) will be worth it. It is the story of victory, the Christian life, and can be the victory story for your home.

****

Let us not become weary in doing good, for at the proper time we will reap a harvest if we do not give up. (Galatians 6:9)

Week 5

April 29 - May 5 – Payson, AZ to Springerville, AZ
134 Miles

Entering Second Month of the *Walk*

Healthier Walking

I walked from Payson, Arizona, to Springerville, Arizona, places I had not known before the *Walk*, but now hold special places in my heart. During the week, we heard there was a serious fire threatening homes in Newbury Park while we walked hundreds of miles away in Arizona.

Week five would take us to the edge of Arizona, preparing us to walk into New Mexico in week six. It was a healthier week of walking, implementing the suggestions from Kecia Davis, my "walk trainer." It was a long week with a lot of walking in desolate, but special places.

A "Reality Show"

Reality shows on television are popular as people seem to want to see "real life." I am not sure that those same people would want to "live" real life, but they want to see it. Our *Walk* could have been a "reality show." It was "real life."

Glenda expressed it best when asked, "What is it like walking across America, living together for six months in a 22-foot RV?"

She answered, "It is kind of like wallpapering together for six months."

If you have wallpapered together, you already know what it means. If you haven't, she meant that even the best of marriages face challenges while doing something like the *Walk* across America. Yes, we had wonderful times, but also challenging times. The following **excerpt** tells a lot.

Glenda and I are having an issue this morning trying to decide where I can walk and where I cannot walk. I have already walked in some places where there was no shoulder, and I had to walk on the side of the road with my ankle tilted too much. The road was sloped, causing my ankle to be tilted at a 45 degree angle to the left, pulling on those tendons and ligaments. That might have damaged them last week. Today, I am balking at walking where there is no pavement or at least a shoulder of some kind.

Glenda wants to be honest with people that we are actually walking across America. My heart is desperately wanting to walk, but my body is also saying be careful—I could end up not walking for two weeks or worse if I mess it up again.

It is one of those little trip issues, little obstacles that we will encounter along the way. We will work it out as we try to get in sync together. The challenges of walking with Jesus across America are the same challenges we face walking with Jesus daily, in our lives, in marriages, and in our homes. That is why we really have to be surrendered to Him.

Everybody has to be putting Jesus first in order to make life what He wants it to be.

We worked things out, but the above excerpt represents some of the challenges we faced while on the *Walk*. People praised us on Facebook for our "wonderful marriage." We do have one, but it is real. We struggle at times. We are two individuals, each with very strong personalities.

On this *Walk,* I had my "game face" on daily. Since I believed I had been called by God to walk across America touching hearts and homes for Him, I was simply doing my best to obey Him every day. Focused and driven, I was not always the easiest to work with, and Glenda was often tired, not getting enough sleep, ever. Challenges, yes, we had them.

Regardless of the challenges, our marriage is extremely strong because we each have put Jesus first in our individual lives and in our marriage. That is the key to our marriage, which I think is a classic love story of two people that have a marriage, blessed and built by Jesus. We are walking across America, bringing hope to every home and to every marriage.

Put Jesus first in your life and your marriage. Surrender to Him daily, and He will make the difference in your life, your marriage, and your home.

Glenda and I love each other and enjoy a wonderful marriage. I have often said that I would love for people to have even half the marriage that we enjoy. It would bless them richly.

Rick and Tammy Rose

On Tuesday, April 30, Rick Rose (who had been with us in Phoenix) joined me to walk four miles west of Heber, Arizona. He and his wife, Tammy, own a home in Heber, which they opened to us for a night.

There was no paved shoulder when Rick joined the *Walk,* so he and I walked through rough weeds for about three miles before we got close to Heber. I was rejuvenated by Rick's arrival and enjoyed walking and talking with him. An airline pilot, Rick works with a very good friend of mine, Edgard Mello, who would walk with me later in Missouri.

Tammy, Rick's wife, met Glenda when Rick joined me, and Glenda followed Tammy to their home in Heber. It was a great evening. They offered us a place to stay in the home, bathe, eat, and just relax. We prayed for them and their family, and they signed our "memory quilt." In just a short time together, they became very special to us. We thanked them for opening their lives and home to us on our *Walk* across America.

Surprise...Surprise: A Memorable Moment!

About 10:00 a.m. on Wednesday, May 1, on a lonely two-lane Hwy 60 in Arizona, I was stunned by somebody coming up behind me. I met very few walkers, and I don't think I had anyone out on the highways ever walk behind me to pass me. It happened that morning.

I was just finishing quoting some Bible verses out loud, when I heard a voice behind me say, "What are you talking about?"

Turning around, I was shocked to see our son, Jared, who lives in Utah. Jared had driven to "surprise us," bringing Glenda an iPhone to help expedite getting pictures to him for Facebook. What a surprise and what a treat to have one of our kids join us on the *Walk*. With their families, work, and busy lives, we never thought about or even asked any one of our kids to join us on the *Walk*. Instead, we were hoping and praying that all might join us in New York when we completed the *Walk*, as part of what could be our **Most Memorable Moment.** We never imagined any one of them doing what Jared did.

We savored the moments Jared was with us. He walked with me several miles through that day and the next, and spent the night in our small RV, sleeping on the "dinette bed." On Thursday, May 2, he left to drive home at about 3:00 p.m.

Dad and son walking

Before he left, he saw one of the "dangers" of the two-lane back roads, often used for transporting "large loads." We saw a police escort preceding a "large load" with instructions for all vehicles to get off the road. The "large load" escort vehicle followed, then we saw THE "large load." It was a large "bucket" from some earth-moving truck or tractor that was so wide it covered both lanes. As it approached slowly pulled by a truck, it was wobbling a little.

Jared said, "Dad, let's get out of here!"

He ran down the sloped side of the road with me right behind him as the huge load passed. It was exciting! We were safe, but it just reminded us of potential dangers of the *Walk*.

Glenda took pictures of us walking before Jared left for home, and I walked on rejuvenated from the **surprise of May 1**.

Glenda's Glimpses: Total Surprise

I was sitting in the RV waiting to move forward past Jim when I saw in my side-view mirror, a car pull up. Someone got out and my hand went to the pepper spray. Then I recognized the face – Jared! He came up to the window on the passenger side.

"What are you doing here?" I asked him, totally surprised.

Jared and I had to figure out where to park his car and how he could come behind Jim to surprise him. He was surprised! We were truly blessed.

After having trouble sending pictures from the phone I had, Jared and Jim had talked about getting an iPhone for me. That was the "reason" or "excuse" for his coming. He brought it and got me all set up with it so that I could develop my career as a photographer. Looking for good shots to document the *Walk* was fun. The iPhone let me immediately email it to Jared so he could post one daily on the Inviting America Home Facebook page. Once in a while, I would get lax and get a text in the morning from him, "Picture?" Then I would have to find a memorable shot to take. He was really on top of the media portion of the *Walk*. He spent hours on Facebook and worked with radio stations and newspapers as well. Thank you, Jared, for all your hard work.

An Unforgettable Stop: "The Transfer Station"

We had a rough night on Thursday, May 2. We came to a fork in the road. Glenda was told there was no place to stay there, so we ended up staying at a refuse transfer station—a place with a lot of waste or garbage. A nice man, Don, told us we could spend the night there. During the night we had a scare as our carbon monoxide warning buzzer went off. We opened the windows even though it was really cold, but we could not get the buzzer off. Glenda called 911 because that was what the RV manual said to do, but we had no idea if there would be a response to a 911 call out in the middle of who knows where.

The local fire chief and a fire engine with two young firefighters came, checked us out with a carbon monoxide detector, but found no trace of carbon monoxide. (Firefighter friends later suggested that it might have been the "aroma" from the transfer station that set off the detector.) After the alarm was off, we did not want to camp there, so the fire chief led us to a non-servicing fire station to spend the night. Since no firefighters were there, he left a door open for us to use the facilities if we desired. We spent the night safely and quietly in the parking lot. We did not want to turn the heat on because the detector might go off again, so we woke up to forty-six degrees in the RV, feeling like we were freezing. I put my gloves on, got ready, and walked five miles that morning just to warm up until we came to Vernon, Arizona, a "store stop."

As serious as the Transfer Station experience was at the time, we later realized how funny it was. Looking at the waste station, RV alarm, 911 call, and a fire engine a day later put it all in perspective. It was one of the funnier stories on the *Walk*. We were reminded that the Proverbs 31 wife, the excellent wife could "laugh at the days to come" (Proverbs 31:25). Part of the joy we had on the *Walk* was to step back, relax, and enjoy the trip, sometimes smiling and sometimes laughing. It helped balance our lives on the *Walk*, as well as it does in daily life.

Glenda's Glimpses: More to the Story

I had driven ahead to a small store at the fork in the road. It had a large graded parking lot that looked like a potential place to park for the night. Sometimes, I felt a little bit like a beggar out there asking for a place to park the RV. You cannot always find a prime place to park every twenty-five miles. When I asked if we could stay in the parking lot, the lady at the counter said their insurance would not allow it. That is when this big man, Don, told me he knew a place we could stay. As soon as Jim caught up with me, it was time to stop, so we followed Don down to the site. It was not the greatest, but we figured we would be left alone there. During the *Walk*, we had to trust an awful lot of people. We were blessed with meeting so many trustworthy people. America is full of them.

When I called 911, I was not sure there was going to be anyone nearby that could come. There were not very many people out there. When we were led to the fire station, they left the door open to the station and said we could cook in there, use the bathroom, and even sleep in there if we wanted to. Very nice people were at the other end of our 911 call for help.

"It Is a Small World After All"

After a five-mile walk, we came to a little town (really a store on Hwy 60) and stopped there. We met a lady named Carol, who was a very outspoken Christian. Glenda and she were engrossed in a fascinating discussion by the time I arrived. Carol told us that the owners of the little country store, Midway Station, were also Christians, Phil and Tracy Estill. They arrived to open the store and had a fascinating story.

They moved to Vernon, Arizona, from Ojai, California, which is only about thirty miles from Newbury Park, our home. Phil told us that he knew

Newbury Park very well as he cleared the land for the new development of over a thousand homes in the Dos Vientos area. The day we were in Vernon, the hills around Dos Vientos were on fire, and Dos Vientos was evacuated. Our firefighter son, Jason, was on duty, and the firefighters saved the day. Newbury Park was spared. We were fascinated that out in the middle of "nowhere" we would connect with people who knew the latest on our hometown and the latest on the fires. **It is a small world, after all.**

Phil and Tracy invited us to join them as they prayed over the door of their store so that people who would come through there would know Jesus. They begin every day with this prayer. After praying, we talked with them, spending more time there than I thought we would. It was a great and refreshing stop, this visit out in the middle of nowhere.

They gave a financial gift to the *Walk* fund right before we left. They said they had been keeping it for some special purpose and believed the *Walk* was a special purpose. As we walked, we encouraged people to have Jesus living in their homes. The Estills had a home (even a store) where Jesus lived. What a wonderful stop on our *Walk*.

"I Don't Do Church"

In Springerville, Arizona, I visited the Dome which is, according to the town's website, "the largest wood frame dome in the United States." Brandon, a young janitor, let me in to see it. It was awesome! They play basketball, football, volleyball, and more there. One time the Dome housed several thousand evacuees during a wildfire. It is truly a full dome. It is fascinating that two adjacent towns (Springerville and Eagar, Arizona) of nearly 7,000 people have something this large. I was fascinated by the Dome, but also by Brandon.

Looking for a church to attend on Sunday, I asked Brandon about a good church to attend. He said that the town had several churches.

I asked, "Do you go to church?"

He answered, "No, I don't do church."

I asked, "Do you believe in God?"

He answered, "Yeah, but I do not like organized religion."

I teasingly responded saying, "You would love our church because we are disorganized."

He smiled as we said goodbye.

"I don't do church" touched me, though I had already heard that on the *Walk*. We responded that the *Walk* was not inviting people to church, but inviting people to have Jesus live in their hearts and homes. We were not inviting people to a religion, but a personal relationship with the living God. I did not share that with Brandon that day, but I wish I had.

I will never forget Brandon's "I don't do church." It helped open my eyes and heart to people on the road. My prayers go out to Brandon. Maybe someday I will get to see him again and share more about a relationship with Jesus than about a religion.

"Jesus First" Church

Sundays were always a day off from walking. Sunday, May 5, we found a church in Springerville, called the "Jesus First" Church where we met special people and attended services with them.

We found it on Saturday evening as we drove around. It was located outside of town and featured a nice-looking facility that was built out in the open, not near any homes.

The people inside greeted us warmly. Pastor Larry Hamblen and his wife invited us to join them for Sunday services. We did.

They invited us to return for a Sunday evening potluck and singspiration. We gladly accepted and had fun eating with over a hundred people and singing after the potluck. It completed a great day with new friends.

We will never forget the "Jesus First" Church and their warmth, hospitality, great food, exciting singing, and most of all, their name and their life. They were "Jesus First" Church and they did put "Jesus First." The dream of our *Walk* would be that everyone we met would put Jesus first and invite Him to live in their lives and homes. That is the **hope** of America. As a woman would tell us later in New York City, that is our "only hope." She was a survivor of 9/11.

Glenda's Glimpses: Lost Gloves

I had email addresses for Larry Hamblen and others from Jesus First Church, so I included them on my prayer updates. Sometime later, I received an email from Larry saying he had been at the Midway Station in Vernon, Arizona, and that Tracy had told him that there was a pair of gloves there that she thought belonged to Jim. We had been missing them, and Jim really liked those gloves. Pastor Larry said he could mail them if we could tell him where to send them. It was far enough along in the trip that I knew where we would land in Virginia. Sure enough, Jim had a package waiting for him in Virginia. It gives a picture of how wonderful the people have been that we have met. Jesus First Church was indeed a very special stop.

REFLECTIONS ON WEEK 5

Put Jesus first in your life and your marriage.
Surrender to Him daily, and He will make the difference in your life, your marriage, and your home.

*As we walked, we encouraged people to have Jesus living in their homes as a witness to others. The dream of our Walk would be that everyone we met would put Jesus first and invite Him to live in their lives and homes. That is the **hope** of America.*

******

When God's people are in need, be ready to help them. Always be eager to practice hospitality. (Romans 12:13 NLT)

How do we put **Jesus first**? We are committed to making:

1. **Jesus first in our lives and in our marriage:**
   We surrender to Him and serve Him, thinking, "How would Jesus handle this?" or "How can I serve my spouse?"
2. **Jesus first in our home:**
   We seek His direction, will and desires. He lives with us. The attitude and atmosphere of our home, including music and media, reflect Jesus.
3. **Jesus first in our family:**
   We seek to do what He would do and want as a family. This includes our behavior and meals, as we eat together without electronic media.
4. **Jesus first in our mornings** (then through the day):

We begin the day by praying during personal prayer walks. Bible reading and devotions come early daily.

5. **Jesus first in our week:**

   We go to church every week to serve and love it.

6. **Jesus first in our finances:**

   We give a tithe (10 percent) of our income to the church, and offerings after that.

7. **Jesus first in our plans and future:**

   We pray about where to work, live, and travel. We seek to listen to His "still small voice" and obey. The *Walk* across America was His call. We obeyed.

8. **Jesus first in our thoughts all day long:**

   His presence (the Holy Spirit) is with us at all times and takes us through the day. Every day ends with us praying together for family and others.

9. **Jesus first when we "mess up":**

   We ask Him to forgive us and ask each other to forgive.

10. **Jesus first in our goal setting:**

    Our number one goal is to **get our family to heaven.**

Have we arrived? No, but Jesus is always there to encourage us, forgive us, renew us and strengthen us by His grace.

Week 6

May 6-12 – Springerville, AZ to Albuquerque, NM
134.9 Miles

"Never Alone!"

Rising to 8,000 feet

It was a week of change, moving us one week closer to New York City, "one step at a time." We were one week closer to our *Most Memorable Moment*, which I still would not allow-in my mind as it was so far away. However, in New Mexico I had time to think, so my vivid imagination came alive.

We saw the high plains of New Mexico. I walked at elevations of 5,000 feet and above, but we were on the plains. Mile after mile it was flat with a few mesas and rises. We saw some cattle, deer, and antelope, but very few cars and fewer people. In one stretch of thirty miles, we saw no houses or evidence of people living there.

It was during this thirty-mile stretch, I remembered people saying that I should skip sections like this because our *Walk* was about people and there were no people there. I did not listen to audio books or music. My phone had no reception, so I could talk to Glenda via walkie-talkie and that was it. I thought to myself, *I wonder if it is a waste of time to walk these thirty miles.*

It was then that a "flash thought" hit me, "Is it a waste of time to walk thirty miles with Me?"

Knowing immediately where that thought came from, I said, "Oh no, Lord. These thirty miles will be priceless."

They were, and I was reminded of one of the main messages of the *Walk*. "Never once did we ever walk alone."

This Walk belonged to Jesus, and He was with me every step of the way. We had a great walk together, especially in the high plains of New Mexico.

We left the high plains to higher elevation, reaching a surprising 8,000 feet during the week. My feet and legs were fine during this climb. I felt good. The air was clear and the beauty of New Mexico was astonishing. Surprisingly, we did not expect such beauty on this road, but we loved it.

Lots of gravel left over from the winter road treatments during snow and ice on the shoulders of the roads meant lots of rocks in my shoes. What do you do when you get a rock in your shoe? You take it out. It slowed me down, but my feet were much happier. It pays to have "happy feet" when you are walking over 3,000 miles.

Red Hill, New Mexico – Population 1

We saw the population on the road information sign and wondered. Glenda drove ahead and phoned me to describe Red Hill. She said it was small, though I had already guessed that. No Walmart. I guessed that, too. It had a house and what seemed to be a mail-drop station.

When I walked into "town," Glenda was visiting with two people in a car who lived in the nearby area, but had come to get their mail. Only one person was counted as a resident in Red Hill. He also was there when I arrived and gave us permission to park in his yard. He said it would be safe and quiet. Quiet was an understatement. It was a great stop for us, and gave us the privilege of meeting a whole town at one time.

Glenda's Glimpses: Moo-ving Experience

What was interesting was that we had seen this man at the Midway Station a few days before. He and a friend had ridden in on motorcycles. The cars were so few and far between that I decided to time them. Generally, there was a car about every five minutes. A couple times there were twenty minutes between one car and the next. No traffic jam here. No "eye in the sky," either.

Pulling out to park and wait for Jim was more of a trick than you would think. Many times, I would stop the RV in the middle of the road, get out and walk on the shoulder to see if I could park. The shoulders tended to be soft, and I did not think it was a good place to have to call for help.

Every once in a while, there would be what I called a short little service road – maybe more like a driveway to a fence. I got a bright idea! Since cars were so infrequent, I thought I would pull out across the road and back onto one of these little service roads right up to the fence. It took a little maneuvering, but I was getting better at it. This made it so I could see Jim for a long ways, and I figured I could have more of an uninterrupted quiet time with the Lord, or so I thought.

As I was reading my Bible and studying, I heard, "Moo." Then I heard another, "Moo." Then, I heard more moos which grew in intensity in sort of an insistent chorus. Wondering what was going on, I got out and looked back at the fence where there was a herd of Black Angus cattle. Grass was dry so they had congregated because they thought I had come to feed them. All I could do was apologize knowing what a disappointment I was to them.

Sorry, cows! No hay today.

Jim called me after I had driven away and told me he saw the cows slowly walking away with their heads down as though they were in depression. When he added it made him consider going into "cow counseling," I just laughed saying the "Moo episode" was a highlight for both of us.

Pie Town, New Mexico...Famous for Pies and Elk?

While walking in places with few towns and people, it amazed me how special "little things" became. Pie Town, New Mexico, was one of those "little things" very new to us. As I walked, I kept seeing signs for Pie Town and for elk. Although I kept looking and hoping, I saw no elk. Meanwhile, I was thinking about pies and wondering if Pie Town really did have pies. Glenda informed me that Pie Town had an RV place where we could spend the night. That sounded good to me.

The threat of rain hovered over us, but no rain and no elk. Would it be the same with the pies?

After 24.6 miles of walking, I arrived at the RV place where Glenda and I worked together to level the RV for the night. Then we shared the two pieces of pie Glenda bought for our dessert after supper. We each enjoyed part of the pecan pie and part of the Mexican apple pie with green chili peppers, both very unique.

Up early, walking away from the RV place, I saw them. No, not pies, but elk. There was a whole herd of them—five, ten, and twelve, maybe more. WOW! Even though I quietly walked closer to them, they ran. However, I finally saw elk!

Glenda's Glimpses: Crossroads

Pie Town was different than I expected. They were not unaccustomed to hikers and bicyclists. They actually had a hiker's hostel in town because people passed through going North/South on the Continental Divide National Scenic Trail. They had seen others who were walking, jogging, and bicycling East/West across America. It was a crossroad that did indeed serve many varieties of unique pies.

Does It Rain in New Mexico?

On Thursday, May 9, I wrote in my daily **journal:** *Beautiful walk through the mountains today as I crossed the 8,000 feet mark. Wow! I wore my blue Poncho for a while with the threat of rain, but no actual rain fell today.*

On Friday, May 10, one day later, I wrote:

What a day! God, the Mover, moved us to Socorro through a thunder and lightning storm that hit while we visited the Very Large Array (VLA) of Radio Telescope Observatory out in the Plains of San Agustin after I had walked fourteen and a half miles. After we saw the VLA, I walked two miles in the rain until the lightning hit. Then we drove through Magdalena to Socorro in a severe storm. Rain was so heavy at one point that we slowed to a crawl in the RV because we could not see twenty feet in front of us.

Yes! It does rain in New Mexico. We saw it and walked in it until the lightning was close. One of the Rules for the *Walk* (see Appendix B for all the Rules for the *Walk*) was that I would not walk when lightning was close. I "walked the miles in a town later," to make up for the miles we drove. This very *rarely happened*, but we called them "bank miles" which were actual miles that I walked to make up for a stretch we had to skip for safety or weather. (I walked "bank miles" in a town, in a Walmart, or anywhere I could walk after we stopped for the day.)

That was the first time rain and lightning happened on the *Walk*, but it would not be the last.

Repairs and Changes: "Life happens on the road."

Was the Lord in charge of this Walk? Yes, absolutely!

In Socorro, I noticed a gouge in the back rear tire. It needed to be changed, but since it was Saturday, all tire stores there were closed. Our son, Andrew, phoned ahead for us as we drove to Albuquerque to keep an appointment. He found a Big O tire store that would service an RV on Saturday. Stopping there to change the tire, we discovered that a Verizon store *just happened* to be a mile away. We changed phone coverage from AT&T to Verizon. We changed because Verizon had better coverage in remote areas.

Days like this further convinced me that this "moving us in rain and lightning" to Socorro was not a coincidence. It was the moving of the Lord to help us with repairs and changes. The *Walk* was like life. Things happen on the road of life, and we need to respond and make "repairs and changes." I was always amazed to see how many aspects of life occurred on the *Walk*.

Glenda's Glimpses: Texting

The phone was very important to me. There were times that the texting from the kids kept me going. All five of our kids and their spouses were on a group text. Sometimes, there was a lot of silliness going on, but it was just the lightheartedness I needed. I needed to hear from them. I needed to hear them connecting to me, to us, and to one another. There are tears in my eyes as I remember and type this. Thank you, kids!

Dr. Will Summers—Neuroscientist

We met Dr. Will Summers, a neuroscientist, in Albuquerque for dinner on Saturday, May 11, at a local restaurant. A neighbor of Dr. Summers joined us for dinner, and Glenda and I thoroughly enjoyed our time with these new friends. After the engaging and enjoyable dinner, Dr. Summers led us to his office building and gave us permission to park our RV in his parking lot.

Since I teach Marriage and Family Life for TCM International Institute, a graduate seminary serving ministers throughout Eastern Europe and Central Asia, Dr. Summers gave me a copy of a book on marriage that he had written.

It was a great evening, after a very long day, but a day blessed by the Lord Jesus in so many ways. We rested that night so thankful for the blessings of the day.

Blessed by an RV Park Gift

Sunday, May 12, was Mother's Day, and we stayed at an RV park on the outskirts of Albuquerque. It was hard for Glenda to be gone from the family on Mother's Day, but it was one of the sacrifices she had made. However, what happened at the RV park lifted her spirits. As Robyn, the hostess of the park, listened to Glenda tell about the *Walk* and why we were doing it, she gave us complimentary lodging. She also signed the *Walk* quilt. We were so blessed by this "surprise gift" which came to us at a needed time.

REFLECTIONS ON WEEK 6

Was the Lord in charge of this Walk? Yes, absolutely!

This Walk belonged to Jesus, and He was with me every step of the way.
We had a great walk together, especially in the high plains of New Mexico.

It was a great evening after a very long day, but a day blessed by the Lord
Jesus in so many ways.
We rested that night so thankful for the blessings of the day.

Never once did we ever walk alone. I was always amazed to see how many
aspects of life occurred on the Walk and called them, "lessons of life seen and
experienced on the Walk."

****

Do not be afraid or discouraged, for the LORD will personally go ahead
of you. He will be with you; he will neither fail you nor abandon you.
(Deuteronomy 31:8 NLT)

Week 7

May 13-19 – Albuquerque, NM to Ft. Sumner, NM
158 Miles

Week of Miles

Edgewood Walmart – The Best

O ur first stop after leaving Albuquerque was in Edgewood, New Mexico, a new and growing development with a huge, new, and extremely clean Walmart. When I commented to one of the store managers how neat and clean everything was in the store, he thanked me. He informed me that this was not only one of the newest Walmart stores, but one of the largest stores, ranking as either the seventeenth or eighteenth largest in the nation. (That ended up being the best Walmart we saw on the *Walk.*)

We dry camped in the parking lot of the Walmart that night, going to bed about 10:45 p.m. after walking 26.2 miles for the day. After the day of walking, I wrote in my **journal** that *the waiter at the Mexican restaurant where we ate was so nice and friendly.* However, being so tired, we did not even get his name to pray for him at the close of the day.

Most Memorable Moment

Walking ten hours a day through New Mexico gave me time to think about the conclusion of the *Walk* in New York City. Lots of ideas and words started bouncing around in my mind. I could not put them together yet, but things like "family," "crossing a bridge," "walking into Times Square," "close friends," "celebration," and "tears of joy" were surfacing.

Getting close to something meaningful, I was going over a sermon one day in preparation for preaching on a trip home. Yes, I preached to the cows and the sagebrush. As I preached about the family crossing a bridge together, tears came and I got so emotional I could not talk. Evidently, I was close to something, though I didn't yet know what it was – I could feel it was coming. I will share more later as that *Most Memorable Moment* grew to become an incredible reality for Glenda and me. It was to be one we would never forget.

Encino, NM - "It's Not What You Might Expect."

Wednesday, May 15, was a simple day. From Clines Corner to Encino, New Mexico, I walked 27 miles on a lightly traveled divided highway. Walking against traffic, I had to cross over the highway divider whenever I stopped for breaks in the RV. Glenda made her frequent stops at "pull outs" along the way, and we made contact by phone or walkie-talkies when phone coverage was not good.

The destination for the day was Encino. I imagined a small, quaint town, full of nice people, vintage small stores, and a unique small diner where the community met at night.

My imagination was influenced a little by the name Encino, the same as the one in Los Angeles area. Before the *Walk*, I had conducted a funeral at Forest Lawn Cemetery with the reception at a home in Encino. The homes were elegant and the people were so friendly. I was anxious to get to the Encino in New Mexico, maybe something like the California Encino. I had hopes.

As the day was drawing to a close, I could see Encino in the distance, miles away. Realizing I was getting close, my walking sped up as it often did at the close of the day. By that time I had walked for hours, my leg muscles were stretched and strong. My normal walking pace of 3.0 to 3.2 mph changed to 3.8 or 4.2. Filled with anticipation, I had Glenda drive into town to "check it out." She did and came back with a brief report.

"It is not what you think."

What did that mean?

She would not tell me, just smiled and said, "You'll see."

Driven more, I pressed on and could not believe what I saw as I arrived in Encino. The town had homes and a population of ninety-four. It had a village hall and a fire station. That was about it. There were no stores and no restaurants, but there was a fire station, city hall, and homes, with several homes that had collapsed. There was also a tiny Roman Catholic Church.

Once in Encino, I jumped in the RV and drove us around the village. It did not take long. While driving down a side street, I noticed we were being followed by two people in a white car. Seeing people erased my thought that I was driving in a "ghost town." Slowing the RV down, the white car pulled up beside us and the driver asked if we needed help. He turned out to be the mayor, John G. Phillips. Welcoming us to Encino, he explained that the village had no restaurant, stores or RV camps, but he offered to let us park behind the village hall and provided power and water hookups. It was wonderful. We camped there and had a private evening and wonderful dinner in our RV.

Encino was not what I expected, but it was a nice little village and a peaceful stop for the night. It had seen better days, but was not done, yet. Without being on a major highway or having industry for work, small towns like Encino struggled to stay alive. However, with dedicated people like the mayor, this village still functioned and served as a nice stop for us on the *Walk*.

Glenda's Glimpses: Small-Town America

We stopped in Vaughn, New Mexico, hoping to get a few groceries, but there wasn't a grocery store. There was a nice hotel and a diner. There was a gas station that had a small market in it, so I visited with the clerk, asking where she bought groceries. She said she would drive an hour and a half to get them and added she was raised there and spent little time elsewhere.

She told me, "I wouldn't live anywhere else," typical of small-town America.

While there, we stopped at a church and visited with the minister. He had a long story of how he had been in the corporate world for many years. After the company had downsized, he felt God calling him into the ministry. We decided to take him to the little diner for dinner. His wife would not be joining him in Vaughn until they sold their house in Georgia. Pastor Roy Denton told us about the town. Both the North/South trains and the East/West trains intersected through town. Apparently, the railroad companies had built the nice hotel because there were so many that came there to work on the railroad.

Pastor Roy invited us to park our RV on his church property that night and provided us with hookups for water and electricity. Another gift provided by the Lord through His people.

Watch Out For Snakes and Buzzards? Yikes!

Walking from Vaughn to Yeso, New Mexico, on Friday, May 17, I had one of the most unique experiences of the *Walk*. It was one of the longest and loneliest stretches of the *Walk*. No houses, no people, just land and sagebrush. I don't even remember any cattle. It was just Glenda and I.

There was no phone coverage, so we were left to communicate only with our walkie-talkies. Trouble was that they were not helpful if she was over a mile away.

On one such stretch, I could see Glenda ahead of me in the RV, but she must have been over a mile away because I could not get her on the walkie-talkie. During that stretch, a car approached me from the opposite direction so I moved over to the side of the road.

The car stopped and the female driver said, "Watch out for rattlesnakes. They are all over out here." As she drove away, I saw a sheriff sticker on the back of her vehicle making me think she must be official.

Concerned, I looked all around, but saw no snakes. In fact, on the entire *Walk*, I think I only saw three or four live snakes. Plenty of dead ones, but few live ones which was okay with me. Alone with no cars, people, animals, or even trains, I had time to think. My thoughts turned to what the lady in the car had said about rattlesnakes.

What if I were bitten by a poisonous snake? Glenda and I had been trained in CPR class how to handle a snake bite, but I could not for the life of me remember what to do. It did not help that when I tried to contact Glenda, I got no answer. Alone, my mind really got busy doing the "what ifs."

What if a snake bit me while I was here alone and out of contact with Glenda? What if I were in trouble? What if I had no contact with anyone? Trying to calm my racing thoughts, I devised a plan to run to Glenda, hoping she saw me coming and would back up to me if I felt I was really in trouble. However, what would we do then? It was at least thirty miles to the nearest town. These small towns seldom had medical facilities. Thinking while watching out for snakes, I was now walking in the middle of the road to avoid any snakes.

It was then that I looked up and saw birds circling over me. Not just any birds, either, these were buzzards. Not funny at all. Rattlesnakes? Isolation? Now buzzards that look for dead bodies to consume? Walking faster now, I finally reached Glenda, glad to still be alive.

We talked, and I calmed down, but we made sure the rest of the day we had contact. Neither of us could remember our First Aid training, so I decided to walk only on pavement and avoid places where the snakes might be.

We made it to Yeso, alive and actually saw no snakes. The "scare" did provide some strange entertainment on the *Walk* that day. Did the Lord have a sense of humor helping me through another long day? I don't know, but I will never forget the snake warning and the buzzards circling overhead. So strange, but it was not so funny at the time.

Glenda's Glimpses: Days Gone By

Be assured that while I might be a ways away, I was keeping Jim in sight and could tell if that bright orange coat had an issue. You can see a long ways, and it would not take long to go back to check and see if he was okay. When we got to hills, divided highways and corners, I would go back from time to time to check on him. I loved those "crossovers" on the divided highways as they made it easy to make a U-turn. Out here, though, it was just a matter of turning around in the road.

We had not been able to have any home visits for a while, but in Yeso we did get to have a "yard" visit. Yeso was smaller than Encino. There was a nice little Post Office so we thought maybe we could camp in the parking lot, but we needed permission. We looked around and it was like a small ghost town. The buildings were actually picturesque with the way much of the stucco had fallen off and left stonework.

We saw two houses that seemed to have someone living in them—one on each side of the highway. One of them had a sprinkler going and a man sitting in his garage. We went over and asked him for permission to stay in the Post Office parking lot. Then we started chatting and he told us a little about the community and how the young people would leave and never come back because there was nothing to keep them there. He said the reason for the dilapidated buildings not being torn down was that they belong to families, and unless they got permission from every member of the family, they could not be torn down.

Our new friend in Yeso

We asked him about his family. With teary eyes, he said that his wife had passed away and his kids had moved away. There was an older widower who lived across the road, but he went to bed very early. We talked about life and why Jim was walking. We talked about how vital it is to have Jesus in the home. He nodded in agreement.

We did not talk with the masses out here. We talked with a gentleman Jesus knows by name. That is just as important.

REFLECTIONS ON WEEK 7

We did not talk with the masses out here.
We talked with a mayor and his wife trying to save their abandoned town.
We talked with a minister answering God's call in the middle of nowhere.
We talked with a widower Jesus knows by name.
They are all important to Jesus.

The Walk belonged to Jesus. He called. He led. He provided. He worked things out for us. We saw the hand of God all over the Walk. We saw the amazing timing, open doors, and met so many wonderful people all along the Walk across America. We trusted Him and have seen His timing and provision throughout our life walk with Him.

****

"Are not two sparrows sold for a penny? Yet not one of them will fall to the ground apart from the will of your Father. And even the very hairs of your head are all numbered. So don't be afraid; you are worth more than many sparrows." – Jesus (Matthew 10:29-31)

Week 8

May 20-26 – Ft. Sumner, NM to Amarillo, TX
109.8 Miles

Week of Milestones

BGEA Team

On Monday, May 20, Glenda and I stopped at an RV park and hooked up the RV after I walked twenty-eight miles. Then some "angels," a Christian family connected to our friend, Lorna Thomas, from Newbury Park, met us and brought lots of Mexican food to make us feel right at home.

Glenda and I were relaxing and enjoying the food when Jon Forrest, pastor of First Christian Church of Clovis, arrived to visit. Glenda had contacted him earlier to tell him about the *Walk,* and then I had talked with him on the phone answering his "questions" and "hesitations" about a man walking across America saying he is a minister. Cautious just as I would be, I figured he was probably expecting me to ask for money. I did not; we just chatted.

We really connected and talked and talked after we discovered we had connections to the same people. When we finally ended our conversation, he said he looked forward to meeting us the next day. However, he did not wait, but came to the RV park for a few minutes that night – we visited like old friends. It is awesome how God works.

The Billy Graham Evangelistic Association Video Team #2 (BGEA Team – Kevin Adamson, Tracy Eakes, and Noah Duguid) arrived around 7:30 p.m. They ate, relaxed, and then before we retired for the night, Kevin interviewed Glenda and me. I felt extremely at ease with Kevin and believed tomorrow's filming would be good. Although I knew I would not walk as many miles while being filmed, it was okay since I had walked twenty-eight miles today.

Clovis, New Mexico – Walking with a Friend

The next day, as I walked with Jon Forrest through Clovis, we stopped at The Lighthouse Mission, a homeless shelter that has touched hundreds of lives for Jesus. The Lighthouse Mission was amazing. I was impacted by the stories of lives that had been changed by Jesus. Geri and her husband, Richard Gomez, run the shelter which was very impressive. It was not just one building, but four buildings and "all debt free," Geri emphasized. They took no government money, but lived on the donations of people in the area.

Touched by the shelter, I had to have Glenda see it, so we went back later with the BGEA Team and filmed the shelter (with Geri's permission). Glenda was equally moved.

During the second visit to the shelter, Geri candidly shared that this loving ministry had grown so large through twenty-seven years that it amazed her. She added that if in the beginning of the ministry she had seen what it would become, she would have told the Lord, "No, I can't do that."

Day by day she just did what needed to be done. They made progress and the ministry inched forward "step by step."

We could identify with that. It sounded a lot like the *Walk*. Step by step we inched closer to New York City, doing just what needed to be done that day. It even sounded a lot like life. It is amazing the parallels from the *Walk* to life that we kept seeing as we walk.

Entering Texas—Twice

May 21 was about as full a day as one would ever expect. Not only was it full of filming and meeting many new people, but we reached a milestone of milestones. We crossed into Texas from Texico, New Mexico, crossing railroad tracks with cheering and dancing for the camera because Glenda and I were so excited. We reached 1,000 miles of walking as I walked into Texas.

Glenda gave me a huge hug and said with tears, "I am so proud of you." I cried, too. We had come a long way.

We still had a long way to go, but we stopped to celebrate.
We learned that we needed to celebrate on our journey.
It gave us incentive to forge ahead.

However, the funniest thing happened after all that celebrating. We were on the wrong road! We should have turned left at the railroad instead of going straight. So, we backed up and "did it again," being filmed crossing into Texas twice. The second celebration was shorter, but now the filming was accurate.

The correct road.

Filming at Dusk

The BGEA Team wanted to film some of the beautiful fields of Texas. They filmed at dusk and interviewed Glenda and me one more time. This time it was on a deserted and somewhat quiet dirt road away from the noise of the trains. After we had said our goodbyes and prayed with the BGEA Team, they left us and our RV alone on the dirt road.

The end of a good, long day

Glenda's Glimpses: The Day Was Not Over Yet

As a budding "photographer," I thought it might be nice to photograph Jim walking into the sunset over the red dirt. It was just about that time; I had him walk it several times, getting different stages of the sunset. I was enjoying this photographing, spotting good shots. All of that added to a delay and to the curiosity of one farmer, Eddie Smith, who drove up to talk to us.

As Glenda and I just sat chatting and wondering where we would spend the night, a seventy-six-year-old farmer in a pickup truck pulled up and asked, "Just curious. What are you folks doing out here? I saw the filming crew and just wondered."

When we told him about the *Walk* and the mission we were on with the BGEA Team and *My Hope America* of the Billy Graham Evangelistic Association for November, he told us to follow him to his house. We did and met his wife, Jeannie, visited with them and they invited us to dry camp in front of their house. *It just happened* to be right on the road where Jim would begin walking in the morning. We slept well that night, even though we were right by the highway and train tracks.

Glenda's Glimpses: The Next Day, May 22

Down the road a ways, we had a fun night ahead of us. We were looking forward to Amarillo because we would get to see some dear friends, Rick and Toni Johnson.

Before we arrived in Amarillo, they had arranged for us to meet friends of theirs, Pamela and Raymond Hamilton, in Friona, Texas, another small town America. Raymond farmed just outside of Friona. I drove on ahead so that we could start getting set up. They were ready for us. When I arrived, Pamela and her sister-in-law greeted me enthusiastically. I told them Jim was coming right away. We went out to the yard and watched with anticipation.

Soon, we saw an orange jacket through the trees. After he walked into the yard, we chatted, then they told us that their church was having a closing picnic for their Wednesday night program. We were a little too leisurely about getting ready, enjoying our baths. However, they seemed to be a little more in a hurry. Then we realized that we had failed to change our clocks when we hit the Texas state line. We actually didn't have a lot of time; we were running late.

By the time we arrived at the festivities, there weren't many hot dogs left, but they had saved some. They treated us like royalty, and we enjoyed being in the family atmosphere with lots of kids running around. They asked Jim and me to say a few words. A reporter from the local paper interviewed us.

The picnic wasn't the end of the fun. We so enjoyed visiting with the Hamilton's when we got back to their house – staying up later than we should have. They had a unique place for us to stay in the RV that night. Raymond had a big shed, big enough to house a grain combine and several other things, park the RV with still plenty of room left over. We were able to connect to water and electricity. It was a cozy night. Texas hospitality was doing well.

First Planned Trip Home – 1/3 of the Way

As part of the plan for a successful "long walk" across America, we planned two trips home. The first would be after 1,000 miles (thinking that would be about 1/3 of the way to New York City). We planned to fly home from Amarillo.

The day finally came. It was Friday, May 24, when Rick Johnson, former elder of Newbury Park First Christian Church now living in Amarillo, took us to the airport. We arrived in Burbank, California. Our daughter, Jamye and her husband, Robert, and their two daughters, Emma and Shyloh, took us home. It was fun to see how baby Shyloh had grown – it was so nice to be home with family again.

It was a very busy weekend. I officiated a wedding for our friends, Greg Anderson and Torrie Halas, and preached on Sunday. Eighty-eight families committed to be "Champions of the Home" after those messages. Getting people to commit their homes to Jesus was the basic reason for the *Walk*.

Sunday after church, we were treated to a BBQ at the church, with many people staying to visit with us. The BBQ was highlighted with a question and answer time for Glenda and me. People wrote questions as part of our interview led by our son, Jason. People were interested in the *Walk*.

The "fast weekend" ended on Monday, May 27, with a 5:00 a.m. ride to LAX as our son, Andrew, dropped us off on his way to work. It was great to be home, but always felt good to be getting back "on the road to New York." It was a great weekend and a very good idea for both of us to be with family and friends again.

Our ***Most Memorable Moment*** was getting closer and beginning to tug at our hearts and form in our minds. It would definitely involve family and friends and would be near the end in New York!

Glenda's Glimpses: A Considerate Husband

One of the ways that Jim showed that he has Jesus in his heart is by consideration. He knew that it was hard for me to leave family, so before we began the *Walk,* he told me he thought we should have two visits home during our six-month journey. He embodies what the Apostle wrote about in 1 Peter 3:7.

> *Husbands, in the same way be considerate as you live with your wives, and treat them with respect as the weaker partner and as heirs with you of the gracious gift of life, so that nothing will hinder your prayers.*

Jim is a very considerate husband, caring about my heart. We had many concerns for which we prayed on our journey – timing, protection, provision, and opportunities, to name just a few. I believe that because the heartbeat of Jesus lives in Jim, the Father honors his prayers and I love him for it.

Jesus in the home is vital!

Glenda's Glimpses: My Daily Prayer Walk

One of the things I do faithfully is to walk 10,000 steps a day. I like to go for prayer walks for part of the 10,000 steps. That is difficult when you are in a twenty-two foot motor home all day, so I had to be creative. As I would go from turnout to turnout, I would walk. Sometimes, especially in the desert, I would park ahead of Jim, walk back to him then walk with him to the motorhome and a little beyond. Other times, I walked on a side road or in a parking lot where I was parked. Many times, I walked in a circle at a turnout, so sometimes it took several turnouts to get in my walk.

Glenda on her prayer walk

As I was praying on one of those small turnouts, three words came to me: commit, connect, and care. We have been very **committed** to being together for our lifetime. We put effort into **caring** for each other, and spend time **connecting** about the important issues in our lives. I believe it was the Lord who gave me those three words, all C's, so I could remember them. Later, He gave me the word cooperate, very important for not only our marriage, but for the *Walk* itself.

REFLECTIONS ON WEEK 8

We still had a long way to go, but we stopped to celebrate.
We learned that we needed to celebrate on the journey.
It gave us incentive to forge ahead.

Step by step we inched closer to New York City, doing just what needed to be
done that day.
It sounds a lot like life.
It is amazing the parallels from the Walk to life that we kept seeing.

Jesus in the home is vital!

****

"I must stay at your house today." So he came down at once and welcomed
him gladly.
– Jesus to Zaccheus (Luke 19:5-6a)

Week 9

May 27 - June 2 – Amarillo, TX to Canadian, TX
114.6 Miles

Walking Through the Texas Panhandle

On the Road Again

Before our trip home, my walking was stopped by a "Texas windstorm" on May 23, forcing me to end the day early. We then drove into Amarillo, Texas, where we spent the night with Rick and Toni Johnson, good friends from Newbury Park who had moved to Amarillo. Perfect. We left our RV in their driveway, and Rick took us to the airport on May 24.

Going home to see family, preach, and conduct a wedding made for a great weekend, though busy. It provided a break and that was good. From the early preparations of the *Walk*, we believed it would be a great idea to break the *Walk* into three parts, with us returning home twice. It was a great idea, but tougher than I thought to start walking again after the break. The Johnson's were amazing, picking us up at the airport in Amarillo on Monday, May 27. They were gracious hosts and excited we were starting the second leg of the *Walk*.

We left their home on Tuesday, May 28, driving back to the spot where we had stopped walking on May 23. As I began walking on Tuesday, my spirit was willing, but not my feet and legs. After a little walking, I could tell the time away from "long and hard walking" would take a few days to get back into the groove, but I pressed on.

It helped walking through Amarillo with Rick Johnson for a ways. We walked and talked and that diverted my mind from my aching legs. While walking on alone through Amarillo, I faced a challenge that caused me to forget my aches: tremendous winds, gusting up to sixty mph! I stopped walking at times to keep from being blown over. Tree limbs were breaking near me as I walked. The challenge of the wind diverted my attention from my aching legs. What legs?

It also helped that we had a great destination that day. We planned to eat at a Cracker Barrel restaurant and camp in their parking lot. What legs? Pancakes were waiting! Rewards at the end of the day, like pancakes, are powerful motivators.

The second phase of the *Walk* was started. In spite of the many challenges, I made it, and we were on our way again to New York City!

Some lessons I learned this week were to keep my eyes on the goal, press on in spite of challenges, and not be surprised by how a destination with a great reward made a powerful motivator.

I enjoyed the pancakes at Cracker Barrel more than usual. Did they get me through the day? They helped. The important thing is I made it!

The Night We Ran

In my **journal**, I entered *The Night We Ran* as the heading for May 28. Why did we run? After walking in the horrible windstorm that day, we parked our RV in the parking lot of Cracker Barrel in Amarillo with the manager's permission – then we ate. Though the windstorm was buffeting our RV with strong gusts that night, we went to sleep, exhausted. We were aware of the destructive tornados that had already hit Moore, Oklahoma, eight days before – we were now walking through "tornado alley" in a very active tornado season.

Glenda's Glimpses: Scary Sound Alerts!

Jim actually fell asleep before I did. Our son, Jason, had called after Jim went to sleep to tell him about one of our grandson's baseball game. Getting the brief version, I told him Dad was asleep and could talk later for more satisfying details – a favorite of Jim's. I finally went to sleep then had a call from Rick Johnson, but I was so tired I decided I would call him in the morning.

At 12:30 a.m. a "storm-threatening alert" on my cell phone accompanied by sirens making frightening sounds awakened us. Realizing that was probably why Rick was trying to call us, we called him back. He was watching and tracking the storm which he said was heading right toward us. No tornados had been sighted or reported yet, but the storm could carry Texas-sized hailstones that could be golf ball or baseball size.

Since it was a slow-moving storm, Rick thought we could make it safely to Claude, Texas, and "ride out the storm" there, so we decided to run. We quickly and nervously started getting things folded up and ready to leave, but our slideout on the RV would not go in. We changed fuses with the help of a flashlight and Jim's shaking fingers, but still nothing. We had been advised not to drive with the slideout out.

The slideout had actually refused to go in once before and an RV shop clerk told us to change the fuse if it happened again. He also said that if worse comes to worse, we could drive with it out. This was definitely "worse comes to worse." We chose to drive to Claude cautiously, but quickly.

Jim: It was a good decision!

The light show put on by nature as we drove was awesome!

When we arrived in Claude, we were not alone. Many Texans had fled to Claude as well. After a short time, many left and returned to their homes hearing that the storm had passed.

We stayed. Ironically, our slideout was working again, so we brought it in and slept in "nap places." (We were informed after the *Walk* by an RV specialist that if the "house battery" is low on the RV, the slideout would not work – wish we had known that in Amarillo that all we had to do was to start the generator.)

We were safe that night, but resuming the *Walk* from Cracker Barrel the next morning, we saw the destruction caused by baseball-size hailstones. We would always remember "The Night We Ran." It is etched into our minds and hearts.

It was another example of God's perfect timing and having a friend for "such a time as this."

He Washed Our RV!

Rick and Toni Johnson did so much for us while we stayed with them in Amarillo. Glenda and I slept in a home, bathed in a tub, ate delicious food, had rides to and from the airport, and a warm visit with dear friends. What could top that?

Rick took it a step higher on the "friend ladder" when he surprised me by washing our dirty RV which had not been washed in eight weeks, covering over 1,000 miles. What a beautiful surprise to begin the second phase of the *Walk* with a shiny, clean RV.

Thank you to Rick and Toni, for being faithful, hospitable friends with Rick doing the unthinkable—washing our RV. You guys are the best!

A Texas BBQ with Jake and Rifle

Late Friday afternoon, May 31, I walked through Miami, Texas. Less than a mile from our stop for the night, a jeep passed me, turned around, and pulled up beside me.

Two young men immediately invited me to join them for a "Texas BBQ," complete with lots of beef, beans, and beer. They would not take "No" for an answer. Jake and Rifle, volunteer firefighters, were having a BBQ with firefighters and their families before they had a big annual fund-raising BBQ on Sunday. Telling them I was tempted, but that I did not drink beer, they laughed and said they would drink enough for me and my wife. My nephew, Mark Johnson, who was on the phone with me, could hear it all through my bluetooth.

When I asked Mark what I should do, he said, "You never turn down a Texas BBQ."

After Jake and Rifle drove on, I told Mark goodbye, called Glenda and told her we were going to a Texas BBQ. That night we not only had great food, but a fantastic visit with volunteer firefighters and their families. We even parked our RV in the cattle field where the BBQ was held. It was a memorable night thanks to Jake Booze and Rifle Collingsworth and Texas hospitality.

Volunteer firefighters – Texas style!

Glenda's Glimpses: Finally Found a Place to Stay

The next day we were headed toward a town called Canadian, Texas. Phoning ahead to try and reach a church where we could stay in the parking lot was hopeless because it was Saturday, and no one was in. When we were a few miles out, Jim suggested I drive into town and check it out. It was a small town like many others we had visited.

Driving around, I found the First Baptist Church with someone in the parking lot. When I got out, I talked with a young mom and her mom. They were preparing for Vacation Bible School. At first she looked at me suspiciously, then I started telling her what we were doing and asked if we could possibly park in the parking lot for the night. By then, Angela Black was so excited she called the pastor, Matthew McCurley, saying he needed to come to the church right away. He did come and told us it would be fine if we wanted to park there.

We visited some and then Angela's girls and parents went to meet Jim and walk with him to the church. That night Angela took us with several others to the local steak house, The Cattle Exchange.

Canadian, Texas – Great Weekend

After walking all day, it was a treat to have an enthusiastic welcoming party of five meet me and walk me to the church. The five were so friendly that we became well-acquainted within minutes. Angela and her girls were most excited, and set the tone for a special evening at the steak house. The food was top notch and the company of new friends was even better. The evening was topped with one special moment. The young pastor, serving there at his first church, asked me for my phone number. He and I had talked for nearly an hour, and then he asked if I would say a few words on Sunday in his church.

When he asked for my birthday, I knew immediately why and would have done the same thing with someone I just met without any referral. He wanted to check me out. I gave it to him. When he introduced me to his church on Sunday, he included more information about me than I had given him. I applauded his wisdom for checking me out.

Dinner with wonderful Texas people!

I shared about the *Walk* for ten minutes in the morning service, then Glenda and I spoke for thirty minutes on Sunday night. We had our noon meal with Angela and her girls, Abigail and Arionna, at her parent's home, Frank and Jeannie Belcher. That evening we ate with another family, the Saul family, along with the McCurley's. It was a town and church which became like family overnight. We left on Monday morning, so blessed and refreshed.

REFLECTIONS ON WEEK 9

The light show put on by nature as we drove was awesome!

We had yet another example of God's perfect timing, having a friend for "such a time as this."
We learned this week to keep our eyes on the goal, pressing on in spite of challenges.

A reward is a great motivator when the road ahead looks especially long and rough.

"And who knows but that you have come to royal position for such a time as this?"
(Cousin Mordecai to Queen Esther in Esther 4:14b)

Week 10

June 3-9 – Canadian, TX to Enid, OK
153.6 Miles

Happy Birthday and Happy Anniversary

Storm-Shelter Time

On Monday, June 3, we left Canadian walking east toward Higgins, a small town in the Texas Panhandle. Late in the morning, a car coming from the east heading west, slowed to a stop. I was used to cars stopping to ask if I needed a ride, a drink of water, or inquiring why I was walking.

The man yelled, "Hey! You Jim Buckley?"

When I answered, "Yes," he shouted back, "You are staying at my house tonight."

I approached his car to get more information. The Saul family, with whom we'd had dinner, phoned him to tell him about our *Walk*. He was so interested that he found me, offering his yard in Higgins as a place to camp for the night.

Although we arrived at his home after supper time, Randy and Rita Thompson saved dinner for us. We visited with these wonderful people until a threatening storm approached with a possible tornado. It was storm shelter time in Higgins, Texas.

Carrying our "Safety and Survival" backpack, we entered the storm shelter on Monday, June 3, about 8:00 p.m., praying that the storm would miss us and our RV would be okay. Their daughter and family of three children entered with us.

In my backpack I had food, water, a radio, a light powered by cranking, and other necessities. I also had a seven-inch hunting knife, though I was not sure what I would use it for in the storm shelter. Nervous, but excited, the nine of us prepared to wait out the storm. Not sure if we were to pray, sing, share life stories or what we were to do in the storm shelter, Glenda and I just kept quiet and prayed for our RV.

After about ten minutes the Thompson's son-in-law said, "All clear. We can get out."

Really? I was ready for hours, but the storm missed us, sparing the RV. It did rain hard, but that was okay, and it actually helped us sleep better.

What a blessing to meet and eat with the Thompsons, spend some time in their storm shelter, and realize once again how God had our backs.

Happy Birthday, Glenda

Wednesday, June 5, was Glenda's sixty-sixth birthday, and I kind of messed up not wishing her happy birthday first thing in the morning. However, at about 8:30, I came to my senses and phoned her, wishing her a happy birthday, apologizing that I had not done that earlier. My only explanations were that I got confused, thinking first that it was our son Andrew's birthday, which is on June 10, and that I must not have been awake earlier.

That evening we celebrated her birthday in Woodward, Oklahoma, at Big Don's Steakhouse. Then we camped at a Walmart where we could take shelter if the pending storm hit that night. It didn't.

My Hardest Day?

There were many days on the *Walk* that were difficult – it is hard to reflect on the "the hardest." However, June 8, was one of them, and the day that probably meant the most as it was such a special day – our forty-fifth wedding anniversary. Having planned a "perfect end to our anniversary day" by staying in the first hotel for us on the *Walk,* made it even harder.

We could have driven to the hotel from anywhere I stopped walking, then driven back to that spot on Monday to restart the *Walk*. However, that did not appeal to the "man" inside me who wanted to be victoriously and triumphantly walking "the entire way." The "man" inside was too stubborn at times to think straight.

As the day began, I was certain walking the entire way to Enid, Oklahoma, would not happen. Battling either a bad case of hay fever, or a very bad cold, had made me weak. Coughing, sneezing, wiping my runny nose, and trying to keep my eyes clear so I could walk was challenging. My normal pace of 3.0 - 3.4 mph was not going to happen as I was lucky to force myself to walk at a slow 1.8 - 2.2 mph.

Though I considered stopping, my stubborn "man" inside would not let me. So, I moped and felt sorry for myself, but I kept walking. Surprisingly, my pace picked up to 2.6 - 3.0 mph as the morning progressed. Can you "walk out" a cold, I wondered? I was hoping I could as I kept walking.

Glenda was magnificent with her encouragement, and my energy drinks helped keep me going. She was not pushing me to walk, but knows me well enough to let me keep walking. Making two, then six, then ten miles, I was getting closer to our goal for the day with every step. At fourteen miles, I was getting excited because I was halfway there!

Then the Oklahoma wind began to blow, fiercely. Most of the time, the wind on the *Walk* was behind me, pushing me forward, but the wind that day was pushing me sideways. That made walking very difficult and slowed me down. So, now not only was I fighting a cold, but the wind as well. Being a fighter, I kept walking. (Notice how I changed "stubborn" to "fighter"? That made my male ego feel better.)

In addition, this particular section of road did not have a shoulder, so I was walking in the grass, slowing me down even more. At this point, Glenda had a "Glenda idea." On her iPad she found a side road on which I could walk that might be easier. The only problem was that it was a dirt farm road. That was both bad and good. It was bad in that I am allergic to dust. However, it was good as I walked past cattle, grain fields and farms – memories from my childhood. So I put on a bandana covering my mouth and nose, and walked on the dirt road for four miles. It was one of the best "Glenda ideas" of the *Walk*.

We were four miles closer to Enid. At twenty miles, I sensed the finish line and was invigorated as I visualized the end. At twenty-four miles, I was close to Enid. Excited, I forgot the sick feelings, the tired and aching body, and focused on the goal. Only four miles to go. I phoned Glenda and announced I was close enough to want to run, although I resisted that temptation.

Moving one foot in front of the other, soon I saw it – the *Hampton Inn*. Dirty, exhausted and very hungry, I arrived. Glenda and I hugged, went to the hotel room, and I collapsed in a chair. My hardest day? Maybe, but I think I did "walk out" the cold and learned a lot about the *Walk* and about life. Just keep walking, just keep going because the end is coming, and then you can celebrate.

It was one of the days I was certain Jesus pushed me or carried me much of the way.

Anniversary Dinner

When I finally arrived at the hotel, we had one problem: I had walked twenty-eight miles. I was not only exhausted, but unable to even think about going *anywhere*, especially out to eat. So, I had phoned Glenda earlier to find a place that would deliver.

At the hotel, I sat down, took off my shoes, and praised the Lord that I had made it. Glenda told me of a steak house only 100 feet from the hotel where we could walk to eat. I could not think of walking even 100 more feet. Lovingly she urged me to reconsider saying that she had talked with the manager who wanted to meet us and talk about the *Walk*. I took a deep breath and agreed since it was our anniversary.

We met the manager (who turned out to be the owner), and he asked why I was walking across America. When I told him it was to encourage Americans to invite Jesus into their lives and homes, he got excited saying that as a Christian, Jesus lived in his home. He was thrilled and awed with what we were doing.

He said he was thankful to have us with him on our anniversary. He treated us to dinner to celebrate forty-five years of a Jesus-centered marriage. He also said he was celebrating two people who were being obedient to the call of Jesus to walk across America with a fantastic message of hope.

Steve Harris, the owner, visited with us for a few minutes before blessing us with a wonderful meal and a relaxing and delicious evening at the Western Steakhouse in Enid. I am glad I walked that extra 100 feet.

It was the perfect surprise gift from our Lord through one of His servants on our Walk across America.

We rested well that night in a clean and comfortable hotel in Enid, Oklahoma.

Glenda's Glimpses: Country Road

By getting on the iPad map, I could see what roads were around. As a farmer's daughter, I understood what I was seeing on the map. Many farming areas have what are called sections. A section is a mile square, so off I would go on one of my explorations, which is why I drove 9,000 miles while Jim walked 3,000.

I found a country road, complete with red dirt. It was one that was used by only farmers and ranchers and only wide enough for one car. It was not graded so it was not totally level, but I was able to drive through even when I met an

Oklahoma, complete with red dirt!

oncoming car. Now, it was a matter of convincing Jim. The red dirt wasn't the best for his hay fever, but his bandana helped, so he agreed.

It actually added a little adventure, and he got to see some cattle featuring a big Angus bull. He didn't have to worry about a shoulder because there wasn't any traffic. He just walked down the center of the road. We got good pictures. It was easy to do because I could stop, leave the RV right in the road, and walk around.

Jim was not always as eager to try side roads. I was the navigator, but he gave the final "nod" as to whether we would take my suggested route. Sometimes he did and sometimes he didn't.

REFLECTIONS ON WEEK 10

What a blessing to meet and eat with the Thompsons, spend some time in their storm shelter, and realize once again how God had our backs.
It was one of the days that I was certain Jesus pushed me or carried me much of the way.

It was the perfect surprise gift from our Lord through one of His servants on our Walk across America.
We met the owner of the restaurant, and he was thrilled and awed with what we were doing. Once again we saw that God was with us, even providing a special blessing to help us celebrate our anniversary.

****

Seek his will in all you do, and he will show you which path to take.
(Proverbs 3:6 NLT)

Week 11
June 10-16 – Enid, OK to Bartlesville, OK
149.6 Miles

The Road Gets Even Hotter

Beautiful Indian Country

Walking through Native American or Indian country is commonplace when walking across America. We had already walked through some Native American country in Arizona and New Mexico. Oklahoma belonged to several different Indian tribes, but most memorable to me was the part that belonged to the Osage Indians.

There were two reasons for this. First, the country I walked in was so green and beautiful. As I walked in front of one man's house, I marveled at his beautiful landscaping all around his modular home. As the homeowner drove into his driveway, I congratulated him on his beautiful yard and asked how he got it so beautiful.

Smiling, he said, "My son mows it."

That's it? He added that last year the entire yard and fields all around him were brown. No rain. This year they had twenty-seven inches of rain. No fertilizer. Just rain.

"It grows green, and we mow it."

> *Thanking him for his insights, I walked on thinking what a difference "God makes." Maybe that could happen in homes if we just trusted God to be the difference.*

Professional landscapers could not do better than God's twenty-seven inches of rain. In homes with Jesus living there, marriages and families would be blessed with "God's plan" just like Osage Indian Country in Oklahoma in 2013.

Second, the same man commended the Osage Indians for being good stewards of financial blessings they had received. He gave them credit for managing them with wisdom and great responsibility.

If It Gets Any Hotter

In Pawhuska, Oklahoma, Glenda and I took an early lunch after only getting ten miles that morning and tried to nap, but the heat was too much. I decided to start walking again, knowing we needed fifteen more miles to be closer to Bartlesville by evening.

Also, a reliable source had given us a "shortcut" to Bartlesville by a seldom-driven back road that was only known to the locals. There would be less traffic and hardly any trucks.

I found that all to be true. However, there was an item missing in this shortcut – a breeze. Without the daily breeze that I received walking in the heat and humidity, the walking was almost unbearable, but we still made it to Bartlesville.

Glenda's Glimpses: Sitting in a Driveway

There was such a variety of places where I would park the RV to watch and wait for Jim. One time on this shortcut, the only place I could park was in front of someone's driveway. I mean right across the driveway. We are talking country. I had to be alert and watch to see if anyone was wanting to turn in or needed to get out so that I could move. I always wondered if people saw me and wondered, "What in the world?!"

She Almost Ate the Whole Thing!

On my walking, it was not unusual for me to find a snake or reptile (normally turtles) that had been killed by a vehicle. One day, I saw a small turtle crossing a lonely highway. I grabbed the turtle and told him, "You won't make it. You will end up dead just like your cousins."

He was small so I took him to the RV to show Glenda, assuming she would say, "Get that thing out of here."

When she saw him, she thought he was cute and kept him. They became friends. She found a small container to keep him in, fed him, and let him walk around outside daily. She named him Tommy, but learned through her research how to determine the sex of a turtle. This one was a girl, so she renamed her Tomye. Females have brown eyes, males have red eyes.

One problem was to find food for Tomye every day. We found bugs, but one or two days, bugs were scarce. In the Bartlesville RV park where we stopped for the weekend, I looked all around and could not find any bugs. Frustrated, I reflected back to my boyhood days to think like a boy. Immediately, I looked under a board.

Lifting up a board, I saw a worm, then another and another. Not able to catch the slimy things, I grabbed for one of the three, got it, but realized the three worms were one long eight-inch worm.

Laughing, I wondered what Tomye would do with it. I took it back to the RV, and Glenda and I concurred to just drop it in. Tomye loved it. She attacked that thing and the fight was on. When the fight was over, most of the worm was eaten and Tomye was full and happy. She did not eat again for two days. What a turtle. We could not believe she almost ate the whole thing.

Glenda's Glimpses: Tomye the Turtle

Tomye was my companion for six weeks. I'll tell more about what happened later, but for now, a little bit about her. I had to go buy a little container for her, but not too small. She was a box turtle, about four inches in diameter, so the container had to be tall enough so she could not stand up on her hind legs and knock it over. It also had to be broad enough to give her moving space.

So, how did a turtle keep me company? I guess I was desperate for companionship. Texts and responses to Facebook entries helped, but it was nice to have something alive in the motorhome. After all, I was in there probably twenty to twenty-two hours a day. So, when I was reading or writing, I would look down at Tomye, and she would look back up at me. She would even stare at me.

At first, when I would pick her up, she hissed at me. Then as I cared for her, fed her, cleaned her abode, talked to her, took her for walks at one of the many turnouts, I became more familiar to her. I would set her down and off she would go, so my walk was usually circling her, keeping an eye on her.

She could book it. She would strain her little head forward and take off. More than once I had to catch her before she disappeared into not-so-tall grass. We did have Tomye disappear into a field one time, but Jim was able to find her, much farther into the field than we could imagine. I believe this is the kind of turtle they use to race on the 4th of July at picnics and county fairs.

At first she would take off away from me. Then later on she would take off going underneath me, using me as an overpass. Also, she quit hissing at me when I picked her up. We had become "buds."

Glenda's buddy, Tomye

Rain Breaks the Heat!

Saturday, June 15, closed one of the toughest weeks of the *Walk* because of the humidity and heat. It was a vicious combination, but I kept walking, making progress.

Bartlesville, Oklahoma, is a sizable town and home of Phillips 66 headquarters. I walked around the town and liked it. A new section, east of the center of town, is a shopper's dream with a whole host of stores, restaurants, and mini-malls.

The best part of Bartlesville was that the humidity broke as the sky opened up and the rains came down heavy and hard. It felt so good to have the rain and when it stopped later in the evening, it was cooler. Praise God for "cooler."

Just having the rain gave me hope that when Monday came, the *Walk* would be so much easier.

Glenda's Glimpses: As It Turned Out

Bartlesville was very memorable. It was time for an oil change on the RV, but we didn't know where to go. When a Pawhuska reporter, Kathryn Swan, interviewed us, we asked her if she had any suggestions where to take an RV for an oil change. She told us of a place in Bartlesville, a tire place, and told us that they had done a good job changing oil on her husband's trucks. She told us to ask for Joey.

When we arrived at Bartlesville, we stopped at the shop and asked for Joey. The man we spoke to said he was Joey. We asked if he would be able to change the oil on the RV. He said he would have to check to see the size of the motor. It was Saturday.

Now, this is the beginning of God's amazing timing. Again!

First thing, Joey said he *just happened* to be between jobs and could do it right then. That was good news for walking sake.

Second, I needed to go grocery shopping. There *just happened* to be a grocery store across the street.

Third, Joey said it would take about thirty minutes. We finished shopping, returned to check on the RV, and they had just finished.

Fourth, was the biggest. Joey was going to be gone the whole next week, but he was there that day.

However, the RV was not the biggest reason it was perfect timing. We had to meet Joey personally. We shared a little bit about the *Walk* before the oil change. Jesus in the home seemed to resonate with Joey, but that was the end of that conversation.

When we came back after getting the groceries, Joey shared more with us. He talked about his own marriage, how God had really been working on his heart. He had been away from the church because of being hurt by something that happened when he was thirteen—church "stuff." But there was a man that had worked with the kids who stayed close to Joey through some growing up and challenging times. He was the dad of a friend of his. This man kept investing in Joey.

Divine appointment with Joey Ainesworth

This man had found out recently that he had cancer. He was given a year to live. Just six weeks into the treatments, he learned that his daughter-in-law had cancer, and it was not good. He said that he would rather take her cancer so that she could live. He had just passed away the week before we were there. It was discovered that the cancer in the daughter-in-law had disappeared.

This man was Joey's heating/cooling serviceman. Joey had called him on a Friday to come work on his air conditioning that was not working. Joey's friend said he would be in on Monday. Then they got word that he passed away on Monday. On Tuesday, Joey went in and the air conditioning was working. Joey indicated that maybe this friend had "one more job to do before he left this life."

Joey was very touched by this man, his love, and by what God had done. Joey said that Jesus in the home was what he wanted and that he and his wife were on their way back to Jesus. It seemed that Joey needed someone to talk to and needed a word of encouragement before the services the next week.

REFLECTIONS ON WEEK 11

Thanking him for his insights, I walked on thinking
what a difference "God makes."
Maybe that could happen in homes if we just trusted God
to be the Difference Maker.

This was the beginning of God's amazing timing. Again!

God provided so many blessings through the things we saw, the people we met,
and the way He encouraged us in the little things like a beautiful green lawn,
a little turtle named Tomye, and a story from a mechanic named Joey.

Daily we were being taught about life from the Master as we walked with
Him across America inviting Americans to have Jesus live in their lives and
homes. We were and are amazed!

****

***As it turned out**, she found herself working in a field belonging to Boaz,*
who was from the clan of Elimelech.
(Ruth 2:3b, emphasis added).

Week 12

June 17-23 – Bartlesville, OK to Springfield, MO
146.4 Miles

Redirection and Reunion

Redirected but Not Stopped

Obstacles of the week included bad roads, either small or nonexistent shoulders, and rain. The rain and bad roads prompted an officer to redirect us north to Kansas, a state that took us into Missouri.

Advice for change of route

By perseverance and determination, we met these obstacles and pressed on. Redirected, yes, but not stopped. This *Walk* was going to reach the finish line in New York City Times Square. There would be more obstacles along the way, but we would continue to meet every obstacle with flexibility and perseverance.

We knew we were on a mission that had to be completed. It was by the grace of our Lord Jesus Christ and His daily help and companionship that we continued on day after day, week after week. *Never once did we ever walk alone.* That was the secret and power of pressing on in the face of every obstacle we faced.

The Field of Dreams

Glenda phoned me as I walked on June 19, and said I needed to take a small detour to see a baseball field. It sounded like fun, so we made a detour to a baseball park called "The Field of Dreams." It was a beautiful baseball stadium actually used for playing real baseball out in the middle of the countryside.

What was "special" that day was what was happening there. It wasn't a baseball game, but a wedding. We didn't stay for the wedding, but I was interviewed about the *Walk* by Kelly from an NBC affiliate. When I met the groom, ushers, family members, and visited with a number of people, they insisted I sign the guestbook before I left. It was the first time I ever signed a guestbook that was a baseball bat. I told Glenda as we left, "Good find and good stop."

Glenda's Glimpses: Tight Spots

As I would wander off to side roads to investigate possible routes, I had a few tight spots of my own. Sometimes, I would decide to go down a road to turn around and come back and park at the stop sign, but I got myself into some jams when there was no place to turn around on those very narrow, one-car-only roads. Jim was no help at all – he was out for a walk. Since he was out of sight, I had to figure out what to do on my own. There was usually no one to help guide me, so I would have to get out to check several times and make sure I was not going to drop into a ditch or get into some soil where I would get really stuck.

One time an older gentleman helped me turn around in his driveway. Another time I had to back up fifty yards relying on my mirrors!

Beautiful Campus

June was highlighted by a tour of Ozark Christian College in Joplin, Missouri. Dru Ashwell, a member of the College staff, greeted us and took us on a tour around their beautiful campus. We met several people, including Matt Proctor, College President, who took time to greet us and have his picture taken with us.

Mr. Proctor was in the midst of writing a book that he would use serving as President of the North American Christian Convention in Louisville, Kentucky, in July. He would deliver the first message at the Convention. It was a powerful message featuring his wife recovering from cancer and his six children who all stood on the platform to say, "Thank you," to everyone who had prayed for them during her battle with cancer which was in remission.

Mr. Proctor and Dru shared some of the memories of the devastating tornado that ripped through Joplin in 2011, killing 158 people and leaving hundreds homeless. Although the College was spared, some people connected to the College died and some lost homes. They shared with us how much the College community and the entire town of Joplin assisted those in need in various ways. It was a devastating time, but a time when thousands from Joplin and beyond rallied to help the needy.

Glenda's Glimpses: "I'm your old friend"

Later, on July 9, at the North American Christian Convention in Louisville, Kentucky, Matt Proctor drew us in as he spoke with deep, real-life, family challenges that were fresh in their walk with Jesus. He then painted a magnificent picture of a glorious, powerful Jesus as described in the book of Revelation. Later, I read the following about Jesus from Mr. Proctor's devotional book, *Victorious,* on Revelation:

"This revelation of Christ in all his splendor washes over John [the Apostle] and knocks him face down on the ground. The glory crushes him like a tidal wave and leaves him fighting for his very breath. He is terrified....

"After John falls on his face in terror at the glorified Christ, Jesus reaches out tenderly, puts a hand on John's shoulder and says, 'Do not be afraid. I am the First and the Last. I am the Living One. I was dead, and behold I am alive for ever and ever!' (Revelation 1:17-18a)

"How reassuring! This great big Jesus is terrifying, but he is also comforting. To these suffering believers, this vision reminds them that Jesus is more powerful than any problem they encounter, stronger than any foe they face. When they overhear Jesus' words to John, they take heart:

" 'Hey John, don't be afraid. It's me! Jesus! The one you loved.
You already know me. I'm your old friend. Don't be afraid.
The Son of Man, the Ancient of Days, the Alpha and the

Omega, the First and the Last, the ruler of the kings of the earth, the one who went to the cross. It's me! It's Jesus!'" John Ortberg, *Everybody's Normal Till You Get to Know Them* (Grand Rapids: Zondervan, 2003) 232[1]

This is why the Walk: Jesus!

Business Loss Is Actually a Testimony of Love

While Glenda was running errands in Joplin, she did see the "new" Joplin, meaning some of the "old" Joplin was destroyed by the 2011 tornado that tore through a one-mile-wide stretch of this quiet Missouri town. While she was driving, I continued walking through downtown, which was old, yet quiet and nice, seeing nothing of the effects of the tornado.

As I was leaving Joplin and walking near the city's small airport, I saw an interesting sight. It looked like a large, abandoned RV park that had been built in a vacant field at the end of a runway. My first guess was someone had tried to take advantage of "open space" by building an RV park, but went bankrupt. We had seen failed businesses before on the *Walk*, but this was the biggest apparent loss we had seen. This failed RV park had many storm shelters that had been built above ground. It was unsightly and unusual. No landscaping appeared to be available in this RV park, either. Obviously it was not built well, but was a rush job that cost somebody lots of money. Now, it was an eyesore standing out as a "business failure."

---

[1] Matt Proctor, *Victorious, A Devotional Study of Revelation* (College Press Publishing Company, 2013) 31, 33

It was big enough that it took me several minutes to walk from the beginning to the end of the park. Then it hit me! How could I have missed what I was seeing? This was no failed business venture. It was a mission of mercy, built for hundreds of families who lost their homes and possessions in the 2011 Joplin tornado. These people must have been scared out of their minds to even stay in Joplin, but this was home where they worked, went to church, and where their children went to school.

We learned later that many agencies, organizations and churches responded and said, "We want to help you." They worked in concert with leaders of the Joplin community who were the driving force. Rather than a park for RV's, we also learned that they built this huge park for house trailers where families could live, some for nearly eighteen months, giving them a chance to rebuild their lives and homes.

All the "eyesore" storm shelters built above ground made sense. In addition, we learned that over 130,000 volunteers from all over America streamed in to aid the recovery. Coupled with the Red Cross, many other agencies and businesses, the recovery of Joplin was a testimony of love for and from the heartland of America. It was estimated that of the displaced survivors, 95 percent of them found housing within twenty-five miles of where they lived. Another testimony of love. The abandoned trailer park was just a portion of the tremendous outpouring of love after the tornado.

The heart of America is strong. We saw it.

My heart was touched as I tried to think about how these families must have felt. First, having their lives spared, but losing their homes must have been life-changing. Second, to see and receive the outpouring of love from people all over America must have been a huge boost in beginning the healing process to return hope to their shattered lives. I was humbled as I walked through this monument of love.

It is amazing how a moment can change one's thinking. I first thought this was a dumb investment, but my last thought was that there is still a lot of love in America.

What a country of caring people I saw embodied on June 20, the day I thought I saw a testimony of business loss, but it was actually a "testimony of love."

Glenda's Glimpses: Empty Lots

Jim had sent me on an errand and I was not thinking about the 2011 tornado. As I was driving south in Joplin (Jim was walking north), I saw several blocks of no structures, just some foundations. Then I saw a brand new housing area and it dawned on me that it was where the tornado had touched down. Someone later told us how they would go into town and couldn't figure out where they were because all of the landmarks were gone.

We talked to some about their experiences. One lady's elderly mother was in the hospital. The hospital staff was trying to get patients out, but she didn't get out before it hit, and her hospital bed got sucked to the window. Because her bed turned sideways to the opening, it couldn't go through and she was spared. There were those associated with Ozark Christian College who had not been spared. People throughout the community were affected personally and when we met them, we felt their sorrow.

What a Way to End the Day!

Have you ever made a really, really dumb decision? Well, I did on June 20, in Carterville, Missouri. After completing my walking that very full day, I jumped in the driver's seat of the RV to give Glenda a chance to use her iPad to help us find a place to park for the evening. Driving to a church she had seen was easy. The parking lot was spacious, but no one was there to get approval to park overnight.

I drove around the large lot looking for a level spot. When I saw one, it was the front entrance to the church and had a covered awning. Carefully driving under it, suddenly I heard a noise on top of the RV. The church's awning was not as high as I thought – I scraped the RV's air conditioner going under it. Getting out and assessing the situation, I wanted to back up, but couldn't without damaging the air conditioner. I was stuck!

Unable to drive forward or back, we prayed and then called AAA for help. The next three hours were a blur of frustration, despair, and a wide range of other feelings. Someone from the church came by and we explained our situation. Our youngest son, Jared, had called with good news that the latest BGEA video was on the internet. He was excited, saying it was great. As I explained our situation, he gave me encouraging words saying that someday we would look back on this and laugh. I said "never" and no one was to ever know about this, either. (Well, here I am telling about it, *almost* laughing.)

The AAA man did everything he could, but we were still stuck. He lowered the air on the tires as far as he could without damaging the tires, then insisted our only option was to back out, ruin our air conditioner and the church awning. Glenda and I prayed and prayed.

Through the inspiration of God, Glenda gave us a word picture that had to do with her dad gently pulling porcupine quills out of a dog's nose.

Somehow it all clicked with our AAA man. He stayed on top of the RV as I slowly backed up. Glenda guided us as I drove in reverse and our AAA friend handled the air conditioner.

Miracle of miracles, it worked. After three hours of figuring and working, we were out. I was so thankful as the AAA man put air back into the tires and finished his part. We did camp on the lot that night on an unlevel spot. The air conditioner cover was the only damage, but the air conditioner worked fine. Even the church awning that appeared damaged was "healed" when we backed up. We heard later, that a church leader put in two new screws and it was as good as new. Praise God!

Seeing Family Is a Wonderful Thing!

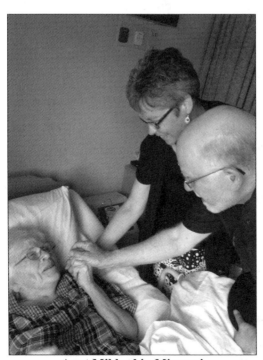

Aunt Mildred in Missouri

On Saturday and Sunday, June 22 and 23, after reaching the 1,600+ mile mark, we had a real treat. We stayed with family the entire weekend. My cousin, Carleen, her husband, Jeff, and sons, Jacob, sixteen, and Matthew, fourteen, were our wonderful hosts for the weekend. How exciting to see my cousin and her family that I had not seen in over forty years since they moved from California to Missouri.

Carleen also had me see a retired podiatrist while we

were there who checked my feet. After adjusting a few "out-of-place bones" in my feet, he pronounced me "good" for the remainder of the *Walk*.

We went to church and then had lunch with Carleen's family at a great burger restaurant in Springfield. Then we surprised Carleen's mom, my ninety-year-old Aunt Mildred, who lived near Carleen in a convalescent home. What a delight to spend time with her. Before leaving Springfield, Carleen's brother and my cousin, Robert Overstreet, also came to see us.

We even joined Aunt Mildred for a second visit and an old-fashioned gospel sing-a-long when we were driving back home after the *Walk* and spent more time with Carleen and her family.

Yes, seeing family is a wonderful thing.

Glenda's Glimpses: *"Jimmy, is it really you?"*

It was a precious time with Jim's Aunt Mildred. What a wonderful attitude from someone whose life had so slowed down.

When we went to her bedside, Carleen told her, "Jimmy Buckley is here to see you."

Jim had not seen her for many years.

Aunt Mildred looked up at Jim as he took her hand, and with a beaming smile said, "Jimmy, is it you? Is it really you?"

She was just so delighted to see him. Oh, that I would have such a joyful spirit as that wonderful eighty-nine-year-old saint!

REFLECTIONS ON WEEK 12

This is why the Walk: Jesus!

The heart of America is strong. We saw it.
What a country of caring people we saw embodied on June 20.
What I thought I saw as a business loss was actually a testimony of love.

*We knew we were on a mission that had to be completed. It was by the grace of our Lord Jesus Christ and His daily help and companionship that we continued on day after day, week after week. **Never once did we ever walk alone.** That was the secret and power of pressing on in the face of every obstacle we faced.*

****

"And if you give even a cup of cold water to one of the least of my followers, you will surely be rewarded." – Jesus (Matthew 10:42 NLT)

Week 13
June 24-30 – Springfield, MO to Winona, MO
154.6 Miles

Time to Sing

Night in an Auction Parking Lot

On our Walk, we daily "trusted the Lord" to help us find places to stay.

Preferred places to spend the night, like RV camps, were not plentiful on the route we took. We had to improvise and be creative. One of the most interesting places we camped was in a parking lot of an auction yard. This was a rather livestock auction yard with lots of pens for cattle, horses, sheep, pigs, etc. We parked away from the main entrance as cars and pickup trucks started coming in the early evening with rabbits, chickens, and a few calves.

We left early before more animals arrived. It was one of the most interesting places we stayed. There was an "aroma," but it reminded us of our roots on the farm.

Most Memorable Moment (MMM)

As we looked forward to the destination of the *Walk,* we began setting our priorities for our **MMM**, including:

#1 - We wanted all twenty-five members of our family to be with us to conclude and celebrate the close of the *Walk* at Times Square in New York City.

#2 - We wanted friends and members of the *Walk* team to join us.

#3 - We wanted to walk to Times Square.

#4 - We wanted to stay together as a family, probably in New Jersey due to cost.

#5 - We learned that we could cross a bridge from New Jersey to New York City, possibly the George Washington Bridge.

What will we do that would be special? We weren't sure, but the idea of the family crossing the bridge still brought tears to my eyes. We were checking out details and **a decision was coming.** Glenda and I were getting excited!

Ouch! Lights Out? Almost!

Most mornings I was motivated to get "on the road." Saturday, June 29, was no different. In my **journal** that night I wrote the following:

Just before leaving Ozark RV, I bumped my head coming up the RV steps, hitting the portable table that had been closed down when I exited the RV. Glenda, needing to use it, put it back up, much to my surprise. I hit it with such force that I went down immediately, lights flashed, but I was not knocked out; just in groggy pain. Glenda encouraged me to get to a medical facility to check it out. Thinking I was okay, I tried walking. At first, I was not at my best, but then I just kept walking. I went twenty-six miles today, ending up at Freemont, Missouri, then back to Winona, Missouri, camping at a church (Assembly of God). I was okay.

It wasn't the first or last time I hit my head on the RV. That explains something, maybe?

Glenda's Glimpses: I Felt So Bad, But Music Lifts Me Up

Jim was so excited to start walking that morning that he was returning to the RV and coming up the steps fast. He really hit his head hard on that portable table. I felt so bad.

From then on, I would **lock the door** of the RV if I had the little extended counter "up" while Jim was outside.

Down the road, I had seen a poster in a window advertising a bluegrass band to play at the Winona Assembly of God Church. I love bluegrass music so I wanted to go!

God surprised us with so much more than music.

What a Church! A Potluck Dinner to Remember

Saturday night, June 29, we slept well after connecting water and electricity to the Assembly of God Church in Winona. Glenda had received permission to camp there after meeting Kristal Derryberry, a delightful young single mom, who was vacuuming the church with a baby on her back. She put Glenda in touch with the minister's wife, Carolyn DeMent.

We woke up early on Sunday morning, and it was very quiet. Services were to start at 10:00 a.m., but at 9:30 a.m. it was still quiet. No one had arrived.

At 9:35 a.m., things changed when a van pulled in, and a lady came to our RV and inquired about the church and how they could get in. The lady was part of the Trinity River Band, the group Glenda wanted to hear. Soon others arrived, and the church was opened. Sunday morning came alive.

We were greeted enthusiastically by Alex Rutledge, one of the members, who introduced us to the minister, Richie DeMent. Alex described him as the man who rode across Missouri on a donkey. Really? This must be the place. They've got a "crazy minister" to go along with a "crazy minister" walking across America.

With a church of eighty people, the spirit was high. The Trinity River Band sang a few songs and was terrific. The donkey-riding preacher preached, and asked me to close the service sharing why I was walking across America. I was delighted to share at the close of such a powerful morning.

The church people invited us to stay for a church potluck after the service which would be followed by a Trinity River Band concert. I've been to a lot of church potlucks that have casseroles loaded with cheese that I don't eat due to my allergies to dairy. This potluck was my kind of potluck. I could eat almost everything – no casseroles with dairy. I loved this church. Since I was walking twenty-five miles a day, I could eat all I wanted. I think I did, too. What a feast! I felt like a king, feasting on some of the best food in the world. What a church, with a potluck to remember! Could the day get any better?

The stage was set for the Trinity River Band, and they delivered.

A Bluegrass Festival at Church?

The Trinity River Band lit up the church with their first song during their afternoon concert. However, it was Mike, the dad and leader of the band, who had already set the stage during the morning church service when he stopped after their first dynamic song and said, "What you see is not what you see!" Interesting beginning, followed by a quick testimony that this "perfect looking family" was not perfect. It came close to self-destructing ten years earlier, and he confessed that it was his fault. By the grace of God, he said the family was saved and now hitting the road to sing praises to Jesus. That set the stage for a powerful afternoon in Missouri. Who would have thought such a day could happen in such a remote place?

We found out that Jesus is alive and well in Missouri!

The band rocked the house with song after song! They *can play* and sing, and they did! It was an awesome afternoon. No "holy nap" that day - just some powerful bluegrass band music to lift our spirits. They were good – very good.

What Next? Hot dogs and Horseshoes, Of Course!

After a great morning at church, with a delicious potluck that followed and a Bluegrass music festival filled with great Christian music, what's next? Normally, it would be a "holy nap," so named by my napping wife to differentiate a weekday nap from a Sunday nap. A weekday nap is about 10-20 minutes. A "holy nap" on Sunday is unlimited. It could be two hours.

Did we get a "holy nap" on Sunday, June 30? No! Not in Missouri. We were invited to go out to Alex Rutledge's home for hot dogs and horseshoes. Did we go? Absolutely! We don't walk across America every day. We went and had a fantastic time. Horseshoe competition was great. I even got a ringer on my first throw—amazing since I hadn't played horseshoes in fifty years.

The hot dogs were yummy. It rained a little, but not for long. The day ended with the Trinity River Band singing a few more songs and leading us all in closing this festive day with some joyous singing.

Jim joining the Trinity River Band

We'll never forget Winona, Missouri, and a day filled with a spirit that would take America back to where she needs to be—praising God and loving one another. This was another one of the small American towns that blessed us so richly.

Glenda's Glimpses: Farewell, Tomye

There are a couple additional details that stand out forever in my mind. Alex Rutledge's "man cave" was first. He invited us in. In it was the studio for his television hunting show, as well as his many hunting trophies. As much as this was a special place for him, his love for the Lord was even more special. The Harris family (Trinity River Band), as well as many others, were vocal about their love for Jesus.

Also, I had been battling with a decision that I faced that afternoon—Tomye. Someone had told me that as we were getting a little more north, we were going to be getting where the winters would be colder and it really wasn't going to be good for my beloved turtle. Also, we were going to be flying home in a couple weeks. I didn't know what I could do with Tomye. Would there be anyone to take care of her? I didn't know if she could survive staying in the motorhome for a few days. I had checked with the airlines and turtles were not allowed in carry-ons. I didn't like her possible future if I turned her loose along the road.

As I talked about it, I realized we were out here, far away from main roads. Maybe it was time to set her free. I kept thinking about it. Finally, I put her in the grass near the bushes. I told Jim what I had done. He was surprised. Then I walked over near the bushes, and I saw her. I picked her up and put her back in her container. All of this was going on during horseshoes and hot dogs. I just kept going back and forth. Again, I put her in the grass near other bushes and walked away. I stayed away for a while. When I went back to check, she was gone. I said farewell to my companion. No more moving her from one spot to another in the motorhome to keep from tripping over her. No more searching for bugs and worms. No more cleaning the container or taking her for "walks," and changing her water. It was good while it lasted. Time to move on.

REFLECTIONS ON WEEK 13

On our Walk, we daily "trusted the Lord" to help us find places to stay.

God surprised us with so much more.

We found out that Jesus is alive and well in Missouri.

We could never doubt that God was with us as He gave us the desires of our hearts time and time again.

****

Delight yourself in the Lord
and he will give you the desires of your heart.
Commit your way to the Lord;
trust in him and he will do this.... (Psalm 37:4-5)

Week 14

July 1-7 – Winona, MO to Cape Girardeau, MO
145.8 Miles

Exciting and Exhausting Week

Cowboy Church in Poplar Bluff

In week thirteen, on Wednesday, June 26, an enjoyable couple, Ed and Barbara Strenfel, stopped me and we talked for a while. I thought it was twenty minutes, but Glenda said it was at least forty-five minutes. Well, we were enjoying talking. They had been married for thirty-five years and were on their way to a "long-delayed" special honeymoon – this one to Florida. They had wanted to go for years, but it just never happened – now they were on their way.

Tuesday, July 2, the Strenfel's were home from their honeymoon and Ed phoned, inviting us to camp at their house. I told him "thank you," but we were all set at an RV Park in Poplar Bluff. Ed was glad we were all set, then he invited us to his church that night.

Ed and Barbara attended Cowboy Church in Poplar Bluff. Our friend from home, Edgard Mello, had arrived and he joined us. We had a fascinating time at the Cowboy Church. Ed was waiting for us, and his pastor featured the story of the *Walk* in his message, having already introduced us to everyone. It was great to be with Ed and Barbara that night. We would be in contact with them again.

After the *Walk,* Ed Strenfel phoned me in February, 2014, telling me that Barbara had awakened from a coma after being on life-support for seven days. She asked to talk to Dr. Buckley. When Ed told her they did not have a doctor by that name, she said, "The man who walked across America." Ed briefed me on her condition, then I talked and prayed with Barbara on the phone. She had been stricken with ARDS (acute respiratory distress syndrome).

Several months later, she improved dramatically, even returning to work. She emailed me later thanking me for praying for her that day. She added that she believed I walked across America to meet them and be available to pray for her in her life-threatening disease. It was thrilling and humbling to meet them on the *Walk* and be a prayer partner during her recovery.

Ed and Barbara are doing well in Poplar Bluff, thrilled to share their testimony that includes meeting a man who walked across America, who months later prayed for her healing in her hour of distress.

A Twenty-five Mile Walk

Edgard Mello, a Brazilian American, is a healthy young man nearing mid-life and employed as a pilot for a major airline. He arrived at the close of the day in time to walk with me part of one day. However, his goal was to walk with me for a full twenty-five miles the next day.

The next day was Wednesday, July 3. I started walking from the RV site and walked one and a half miles to meet Edgard as he left his hotel room. Off we went together for a full day of walking. It was a beautiful day, and the shoulder of the divided highway was huge, maybe 10-12 feet of paved shoulder. It was some of the best we had on the entire *Walk.*

It accommodated both of us. God's perfect timing—just when Edgard would be there.

However, I normally walked 3.2-3.6 mph, but Edgard wanted to walk about 4.0-4.2. I kept slowing him saying, "Slow down. I'm going to New York City, you're not. At your walking pace, we'll both be exhausted by noon. I'll have to recover for days."

He slowed down, but we still made great time. Glenda found a picnic spot for us, picked us up, bandaged Edgard's blisters, and prepared lunch for us. Edgard sat down in our zero gravity chair and promptly fell asleep. After lunch and a brief rest, we were on the road again, walking to Dexter, Missouri.

In Dexter, we were treated to dinner by Dave and Jane Silverspring. Dave wanted to meet us and interview us about the *Walk*. It was a delightful dinner with them. Then they ended up driving Edgard back to Poplar Bluff, from where he would leave in the morning.

When we stopped for the day, I told Edgard we walked twenty-five miles. He was disappointed because he knew I had already walked one and a half miles to meet him in the morning, so he concluded that he had only walked twenty-three and a half miles. Laughing, I told him he actually walked twenty-five miles, but I walked twenty-six and a half miles so he would get his "full day" of walking.

He smiled big, hugged me, and said, "Wow! I can't believe you do this every day."

"I can't either," as I smiled and thanked him profusely for walking the whole day with me. Edgard Mello was the only one who walked a full twenty-five miles with me on the *Walk*.

Jim walking twenty-five miles with Edgard

One More *"It Just So Happened"*

"It just so happened" that Edgard and I were walking when our youngest son, Jared, called, needing advice on airline tickets. He told me of a special on tickets and asked if I thought that was a good price. I asked Edgard, who used a phone calculator and said, "Yes. Buy them now. Great bargain." Jared bought his and passed the advice to others in the family. By the end of the day, all the tickets to New York were purchased.

God's perfect timing brought us one step closer to the
MMM, *thanks to Edgard's quick calculations and knowledge of air fares.*

Throw Me a Roll!

Sometimes in life one needs a change of pace – something special that will break the routine. On July 4, I walked 25.4 miles. It was another long day of walking. For some reason, I resented walking that day. My mind went back to days of working in the harvest field in the hot summers in California. Even then we took July 4 off. We didn't work. We relaxed and partied. That's what I wanted to do, but first I wanted to walk a full day, then party. By the time I had walked, I was so tired and grumpy that when we arrived in Sikeston, Missouri, to stop for the night, I needed something special. I needed a change of pace.

We found one at the world famous Lambert's Restaurant, home of "throwed rolls." We walked into this famous place and were fascinated by it.

Glenda's Glimpses: Black-eyed Peas, Fried Okra, and More

It was a fun place to eat. A good friend had told us about it and said since we would be there in Sikeston, to be sure to eat there. One of the rolls banked off of Jim and I caught it, and I'm not the athlete! As we were eating, the servers would come around with huge stainless steel bowls and big, long-handled spoons to offer us servings of their food. They called them "pass arounds." They served up fried potatoes, onions, macaroni, tomatoes, black-eyed peas, fried okra, hot rolls, sorghum, and apple butter. Does it sound like something from the past? It's a family restaurant that opened in 1942.

The "throwed rolls" started when the son of the original owner was too busy to go serve a requested roll, so when someone yelled for him to throw it, he did. Sounds like something that could happen at your dinner table, right? In fact, Jim tells a story from his own family with five teens sitting around

137

the table that, much to his mom's dismay, that very thing happened. In fact, I remember that happening at a Thanksgiving dinner with my extended family. These are the types of things that can happen at meals around a table where memories are birthed.

That brings me to a suggestion made by Tom Stephen, our neighboring pastor in Newbury Park. He said so few Americans sit down as a family to eat dinner. He suggested that we ask families to pledge to eat a meal together at least one time a week with no electronics—no texting, no news, no TV programs, no phone conversations, no iPad, etc.—just food and conversation. Shouldn't be hard, should it? Is that what is going on at your family's dinner table?

Happy 237!

While America celebrated 237 years as a great nation, we found an RV park, did laundry, showered, and collapsed. We celebrated Happy Birthday America with a quiet night after a long day. Our spirit was really willing, but our flesh was weak. Not age, mind you, but walking nearly 2,000 miles in three months was catching up with us.

Narrow Bridge – Reroute

Most of our obstacles on the *Walk* seemed to be health, road or weather-related. Glenda was talking to a state trooper on July 4, who asked which direction I was headed to cross the Mississippi. When she told him Hwy 60 crossing into Cairo, Illinois, he advised her to take a different route. He said the bridge at that crossing was not a walking bridge. It was also narrow with huge trucks crossing it, jeopardizing our RV as we crossed the bridge.

When Glenda informed me of that news on an already tough day for me, I didn't like the thought of rerouting and backtracking. However, I agreed that we should look at the option he was suggesting. We did and decided to reroute to cross a wider bridge over the Mississippi.

The "rerouting day" on July 5 was special with a brief television interview by a nice young man named Joshua. The interview was aired on a local TV station in Cape Girardeau, Missouri. The interview was prompted by some "grandmas" at Granny Pickers, a very nice second-hand store near Bloomfield, Missouri. The nice ladies inquired about the *Walk* when I stopped to throw away some trash. They phoned the television station. Grandmas must have clout!

Glenda's Glimpses: Television Interview

Jim called me and told me about Granny Pickers and said I needed to come see it. It was a very large, well-organized thrift shop with a lot of "valuable stuff." I even bought a lid for one of my pans. Still use it! Anyway, as I drove on, I had to catch up with Jim. When I caught sight of him, I saw that he was talking to someone in a small parking lot—not unusual. Then I realized that the man he was talking to had a microphone and that there was a television camera on him. I drove up to them just as they were finishing and met the interviewer.

Jim: It was just a short clip that was aired, but I was criticized on Facebook by one man who said I was wasting my time walking across America. I should be home taking care of my family and doing something productive. His short remark was countered by many other comments from those who were so impressed with my commitment to the homes of America that I would "put feet to my faith" or put my "money where my mouth is." The bottom line was that the brief report of the *Walk* on the station's

Facebook had more "likes" than any other news event aired that day on their television station. Interesting! Following is a Facebook response of our son, Jason, to the criticism by that one person to our *Walk*. It was nice to have the support of our kids to challenges we faced. Thanks, Jason, for "walking with us."

I am son number two of the five kids of Jim and Glenda Buckley. I'm now a father to five children, a husband to a wonderful woman seventeen years today. I have a great job, a wonderful church family, and I love the Lord Jesus Christ. I say all this because this sixty-six-year-old man walking across the country is my dad. I have learned so much from both him and my mom about faith, marriage, parenting, and finances. These two are the wisest people I know, and that's in all areas of their life. I'm writing just to say how proud I am of both of you for doing what God has called you to do. Anyone that is in their walking path, go out and say hi to them. If you're not, then pray for them. If you get the chance to meet them, you, too, will see who they are and you will be blessed.

Love you both,
Jason

"Is that blind woman with you?"

Some of the strangest things happened to us on the *Walk*. The story of stories occurred on the day that somebody stopped Glenda and wanted to know if that blind woman was with her. "That blind woman?" I did have a cane (walking stick). I had sunglasses on. I was going back and forth across the road because I was carrying the GoPro Camera of the BGEA Team, filming pictures of the countryside from a quiet country road in Missouri. I wanted to record this for the video team.

How in the world did she ever come up with me being a blind *woman*? The cane, dark glasses, and wanderings? Maybe. I was wearing an XL orange shirt (almost blousy), and I guess I must have a wiggle. I didn't know why, but that weird question will not be forgotten!

Glenda's Glimpses: Tough Day

It was fun to talk to the lady about *my blind-woman husband*. I explained to her what he was doing, why the "cane," and why he was walking back and forth across the road. But we were puzzled, why woman? Later, I discovered why she thought Jim was a blind *woman*. Parked at my turnout, I watched while he walked past me. He was wearing what we called a "bee-keeper" hat. The loose part in the back of the hat would flap in the breeze, so Jim would tie a bandana around the flap and his neck. As he walked by, I realized it made it look like a bonnet and told Jim! He didn't wear that hat anymore.

It seems like there are a lot of holes in the story of this week. I think it was because of the many challenges. There were also many blessings. For one, it was fun to be with Edgard. He was so tired by noon. He laughed at me because after lunch, I took them right back to the spot they had left off. He said that I didn't give them any grace at all. Gotta' stay honest!

Now to the challenges or the frustrations: the confusing road situation and our own emotions. It was really hard for Jim to walk on July 4. When Jim was growing up, July 4 was a day off from harvesting grain for his dad and it was a big family day. It was his mom's birthday and a day to celebrate. Then as our own family had grown, we liked to celebrate it together. We'd barbeque, then on to fireworks together.

We had a hard time finding a good place to stay that night. We had hoped to find a place where we could see fireworks. We had actually passed up "crashing" a church potluck in a local park because we were so tired; we didn't want to be so visible. Then the RV park we chose was not the best. I had a lot of laundry to do, too. Not exactly the way to celebrate the fourth.

Then I realized we couldn't see the fireworks. We were both tired and grumpy! I think I felt so alone in the middle of America because I was homesick plus we weren't happy with each other that day. All five of our kids and their families were together, but we weren't there. The kids decided to FaceTime us. Instead of it being comforting to me, my grumpy self just got grumpier. I tried to not show it to the kids. I even had to walk away for a little bit. It was probably **my hardest day being away from our kids** all together, and the conflict with Jim and me didn't help.

We resolved our tension only to have another hard day the next day with the road. Jim had to backtrack since we couldn't cross where we had planned. We drove back to Dexter over the very road he had walked, then he walked north to Advance, Missouri. Jim was describing where we stayed there and for the life of me, I can't remember. It's all a blur. I remember Hwy 25 up to it, but not that night. This was so out of the way–frustrating for both of us.

We did stay in a Christian Church parking lot the next night in Cape Girardeau. We went to two church services. The first church was big and the minister was telling what the Lord revealed to him about who was in the audience–their various kinds of needs. Well, I guess the Lord didn't seem to reveal to him that Jim was there and what he was doing. He missed such a grand opportunity! See where my head was? Oh, well. We dashed over to the other small church service to get the rest of their service. We had a nice visit, but they had a leaders' meeting, so back to ourselves (in more ways than one). Tomorrow would be a new week!

REFLECTIONS ON WEEK 14

God's perfect timing: just when Edgard would be there, we walked a stretch
of road that could accommodate both of us side-by-side.
*God's timing **is** perfect since He's in charge. He worked things out for us each*
and every day.

****

You see, at just the right time, when we were still powerless, Christ died for
the ungodly. (Romans 5:6)

Week 15

July 8-15 – Cape Girardeau, MO to Anna, IL
28 Miles

Crossing a Mighty River

The Mighty Mississippi—Big and Beautiful

Mighty and majestic, big and beautiful are words that do not do justice to the Mississippi River. It's so amazing that the word "river" is not always placed in conjunction with the word "Mississippi." It stands alone. "We crossed the Mississippi." "River" was not necessary to describe **the** Mississippi.

"**Excerpt** from the road" before I actually crossed the Mississippi: *It is 6:51 a.m. on July 8, 2013, day 99 of the Walk. It's an exciting morning. I'm walking down South Broadway, turning on Route 74 in a moment, and I'll be headed toward the mighty Mississippi. I'll be there maybe an hour from now, and I'll cross the river on a very good bridge. Glenda and I just drove across it to see it so that she would know what she is driving across, because we've heard horror stories about certain bridges. This one is a beautifully constructed newer bridge, and it has a nice shoulder on which I can walk. I'll walk against traffic as I normally do. It's a crystal clear morning. It's cooler, and we're looking forward to a great day with Jesus. We'll be crossing from Missouri to Illinois.*

What a river. As I walked closer to the bridge, I could see the river. It was big and powerful, even from a distance. I was so glad we changed routes so

I could walk across this famous river rather than ride in the RV across it. It has a foot path that makes it walkable. Praise God.

Crossing the Mississippi

We were delayed in crossing the Mississippi due to battery failure in the BGEA Team's GoPro Camera. Around 11:00 a.m., we crossed. I was walking on the north side of the bridge, against traffic as usual.

I jokingly told people *after* I had crossed the river that I had a huge decision to make *before* crossing the Mississippi. Should I cross the river by walking on the bridge or on the water? I chose the bridge since it was somewhat new, and that was a good choice.

As I walked, stopping to film at times, I was simply amazed at the size and power of the river. As I was walking on the bridge and overlooking the water, I sensed an aura that accompanied every step I took across this bridge which is nearly a mile long. It was a glorious moment with each step.

Stopping at times, I just contemplated what I was actually doing and from where I had come.

I began in Newbury Park, California, on April 1, and now on July 8, I was actually walking across the Mississippi River, having walked the entire way from Newbury Park. It's amazing to just stop to think at times about the *Walk*. That moment added to the glory of the morning.

A funny moment occurred when I saw our RV approaching. I stopped to take a picture of Glenda driving across the Mississippi, but was surprised that she was slowing down to take pictures of me. My wife, a novice in driving an RV, and one who does not like driving across bridges, was taking pictures as she drove an RV across one of the biggest bridges we faced on the Walk.

Across the Mississippi}

I laughed, then yelled while smiling, "Be careful."

She kept driving with no problems and met me on the other side as I walked into Illinois. We embraced, praising God for His mighty river and fantastic country.

What an exciting day crossing the mighty Mississippi.
This was a definite high point of the Walk.

Arriving in Louisville in an RV

We drove to an RV park in Marion, Illinois, on our way to Louisville, Kentucky, for the North American Christian Convention after stopping the *Walk* in Anna, Illinois. The Convention is an annual gathering of Christians with their families coming from across the United States and beyond. Thousands of people are inspired by preaching sessions, workshops, Bible studies, and wonderful music.

We drove from Marion to Louisville, crossing the Ohio River twice, arriving in Louisville around 2:00 p.m. We experienced the fun of driving downtown where we stayed at a hotel during the convention. However, we had a question. Where do you park an RV in a city?

The hotel did have RV parking, but we had not counted on so many people bringing RV's and the RV spaces being taken. We did some "should haves." "We should have left earlier." "We should have parked at a church and taken a taxi to the hotel." So, what did we do?

Of course, we prayed for the Lord to help us as He had done many times before on the Walk and in life.

After driving around the hotel several times (which took some time in city traffic and one-way streets), we decided to try some "tricky maneuvering," using RV leveling blocks to go over curbs. With Glenda's guidance (and the Lord's help), I "maneuvered" the RV into the last, tight spot. It was a challenge, but we made it. We left the RV there until Friday morning when we left Louisville for Nashville for our flight home to California to see family.

With the RV parked, we checked into a lovely hotel room which would be our new home for three nights. Praise God we made it to the Convention.

My feet rejoiced, knowing that walking would be at a minimum for the next several days. I did walk, storing up "bank miles" to be used later, but also to stay in "walking shape."

What about the RV in Nashville?

We chose to fly home from Nashville, Tennessee, rather than Louisville because airline tickets cost so much less. However, where could we leave the RV in Nashville? We considered leaving it at the airport and pay for the parking fee. At the airport, it would not be plugged in for four days which presented a problem for our food.

There were so many "little decisions" we faced on the Walk. So much like life.

Our issue was resolved when we were given the name of a man at Christ Church North in Whitehouse, Tennessee, near Nashville. We contacted Rod Vannoy, and he said we could leave the RV at the church over the weekend. He would meet us at the church and drive us to the airport for our flight.

It worked. He met us at the church. After we hooked up the water and electrical, he drove us to the airport in his "work van" in which he made a special "comfort seat" in the back area for me and provided refreshments for the thirty-minute drive. He was awesome.

As often happened on the Walk, challenges were changed into blessings.

This challenge that turned into a blessing was one of the best and most memorable, because more blessings would flow out of it in week sixteen.

Home Again to See Family and Friends – Preaching, as Well!

Sunday, July 14, was a special Sunday as we were home. I preached in both services, but the first service at 9:00 a.m. was extra special. Worship was uplifting, then Pastor Ken led communion and had our son, Jared, introduce me. His words were very humbling and honoring and were a great introduction for the message.

My sermon went really well in the first service, even seeming electric at times. The first service's message was emotionally charged, resulting in many tears. I think we all were in awe about how the *Walk* was a living example of one family's commitment to having Jesus live in our home. The electricity may have been stronger because our family was present, and we can be very emotional. In addition, Glenda and I were on a mission answering God's call to walk across America, but that mission was taking us away from family and friends and was impacting our family, as well as our very special church family.

My exhaustion level told me that I should have rested more during the Convention in Louisville. I didn't since there were so many people with whom to connect. The Lord was good, giving us a beautiful morning at home in Newbury Park. It's a nice place to walk, too. If I could walk across America in Newbury Park, the *Walk* would be a whole lot easier. But it wouldn't be the *Walk* across America then. What a dreamer I am.

Glenda's Glimpses: Family "Fix"

What a good time we had. There was a lot of orange. Our family and others wore orange shirts to church. Even at home it is quite an ordeal to get our family all together. Tina Bumstead, our worship pastor's wife, is a professional photographer. She came to our house and did a photo shoot. It was quite a challenge just getting the whole family to even look the same direction, especially when five of the grandkids were four years old and younger. She took several pictures of the family – the whole group. She then took pictures of each of our kids' families – one time with just their regular clothes and one with their family in orange shirts. It was pretty overwhelming. She did an amazing job!

Smile, Buckleys

We talked, planned, laughed, ate together, and even played, "Ring Around the Rosie!" I have a picture to prove it. It really did this mom/grandma's heart good. The *Walk* is two thirds completed and with this little "fix," I knew I could make it the rest of the way. It's fun to look back at that picture and know that now some of the grandkids have passed me in height. As my mom would say, "That's not really much of an accomplishment." (She was

4'11½"!) Anyway, it felt so good to be with family. Thank you, Jim, for loving me enough to have it happen–he knows me. I want to thank our Father for making it possible.

Preparing for New York City (MMM Preparation)

After family pictures, the older eleven grandkids watched a video while the twelve adults and the two smallest grandchildren joined the adults meeting outside. Each of the adults shared their feelings about Glenda and me as their parents on this *Walk* of faith and their excitement about us answering God's call. They were all open and that was good for Glenda and me. What a blessing our family is to us.

As we met, I could tell we all felt united in power and strength in the Lord. Everything was in the Lord's hands. It has been His trip from the beginning.

We spent time looking over the New York trip (plans for our *MMM*) and all that the trip might mean. Each family would fly in and be there for at least a few days, flying in either Wednesday or Thursday with all being there at least Friday, Saturday, and Sunday. Daniel and Charity might leave on Monday, with the others leaving on Tuesday or Wednesday. After that, Glenda and I would drive home.

Glenda and I told them that we had decided to walk across the George Washington Bridge as a family on October 4. It would take us from New Jersey to New York where friends would meet us to begin the nine-mile walk to Times Square. We decided on that bridge after talking with Kevin McSweeney, who directs the painting crew of the bridge and knows it and other bridges in New York very well. It is a walking bridge, over 200 feet above the Hudson River. We will have tight control on all our kids. I talked to the older grandkids privately telling them "no fooling around" on that bridge. They listened, and even got more excited about the trip and the final walk. A mile long, it will be a memorable walk across the bridge.

They all had their tickets as of that night. Exciting!

As far as where to stay, Sherry and Kevin McSweeney offered their home to us if we needed it. Since it's an hour outside of New York, it might not be used. The family decided they really wanted to stay together, if possible. We told them we were trying to make arrangements housing-wise, but added that it would virtually be a major investment. As with the entire *Walk*, we'd be totally depending on God. He had been providing the tickets. He had been providing things all along. This was His trip, there's no doubt, and I shared with our kids how my heart has just been turned around completely. From my normal tendency to have all details covered, I had to trust God to take care of last-minute details. (He would in awesome ways in our ***MMM.***)

We were praying for God to open up the heavens and provide a miracle to allow us to be together and to have whatever impact He wanted us to have as a family in New York City. This was a prayer for what would become our ***Most Memorable Moment***.

If He can touch a family, one family or one person to bring them closer to Jesus and get Jesus alive in their home, the trip would be worth it.

Glenda and I knew that God had been touching lives all along the *Walk* already. We left that meeting, excited about what God was going to do in New York with His family. We didn't know the details, but we knew Who did know and with that, we rested well.

REFLECTIONS ON WEEK 15

As often happened on the Walk, challenges were changed into blessings.

If He can touch one family or one person to bring them closer to Jesus and get Jesus alive in their home, the trip would be worth it.

There were so many "little decisions" we faced on the Walk that were so much like life. Having Jesus #1 in our lives, our marriage, and our home has made all the difference in our marriage and family.

****

As for me and my household, we will serve the Lord. (Joshua 24:15b)

Week 16
July 15-21 – Paducah, KY to Canton, KY
87.3 Miles

On the Road Again

Christ Church North's Wednesday Special

C hrist Church North wanted us to stay and speak to their Wednesday night service. We accepted. The extra day gave us an opportunity to rest some before we began the final leg of the *Walk*. In addition, we'd have the thrill of sharing the story of the *Walk*, which we loved to do.

Glenda slept in on Wednesday while I was up early walking, getting some "bank miles," plus just walking again. It felt good. Sleeping and resting for Glenda and walking for me.

Glenda: We both knew that accepting the invitation to speak at Christ Church North was what God wanted. It was one of the many times when Jim let go of his push to get closer to New York so that we could accomplish the purpose of the *Walk,* to carry the message of **Jesus in the home.** The church people were very plugged into the message. It was the first of two major stops that week for the message of Jesus in the home.

Jim: The Wednesday night service was worth the extra day in Tennessee. About sixty enthusiastic people attended a spirited praise time. They were so excited and responsive about the story of the *Walk* and the things that

God was doing as we walked. We were blessed by the love and generosity of the Christ Church North's family.

Glenda: When we got back to Nashville on Tuesday, I realized that the BGEA Team that was going to be taping us in a couple days lived in Nashville. I gave them a call to let them know that Jim would be speaking at Christ Church North. It worked out for them to come and do some preliminary video-taping. It gave us an opportunity to get to know them since we had not worked with this crew before. We enjoyed each group. They are all wonderful men of God.

Glenda's Glimpses: Catch-Up Time

Leaving the RV in Nashville led us to God's appointments. Spending a little time with Christ Church North in Whitehouse, Tennessee, was a good decision. It was something I needed personally to let life catch up just a little bit before getting started again. I had slept much of the flight back, but I needed more. I got to sleep a little extra and have some lingering quiet time with the Lord and not have to drive.

On the Road Again – Yay!

We drove back to our starting point in Paducah to resume our walk and actually begin the final leg of the *Walk*. I woke up before the alarm (not unusual) and was extremely excited.

Yay! Let's go!

I taped my ankles, put on my walking socks, and then my ankle support. I could feel the excitement growing. After my long-sleeved UnderArmour and neon orange, "I'm Walking Across America" shirts were on, I put on my walking pants, my shoes, and my "war paint" (sun block) on my face. I ate my cereal while reading my Bible and entering things in my daily journal. After I had my protein drink, I put on my Garmin watch, then my belt with the cell phone and mini-recorder attached. Glenda was also getting ready.

With my two pedometers (one in each pocket), Blistex, Bluetooth, and glasses, I grabbed my wide brim hat and my sticks, and said to Glenda, "Let's pray." We prayed and out the RV door I went. It was sunlight outside, and I was walking.

Oh, was I excited to be "on the road again." Yes, I loved the Convention, being home, preaching, spending time with family, and speaking at Christ Church North. But I was on a mission to walk across America and to invite

America to have Jesus living in every home. Neither mission was yet complete, but we were two thirds complete on the *Walk* mission, and making a dent on the second part of the mission.

I had to walk south for a while then east where we finally landed in Farmington, Kentucky. Yes, I was tired, but it was a great feeling to be "on the road again" on our mission to *Walk* across America. We were one day closer to New York. I slept well that night knowing we were moving closer to our destination one step, one day at a time.

"Oh, and would you preach on Sunday?"

Glenda was busy on Friday, July 19, talking with a minister of a church in Canton, Kentucky, about parking our RV on their church property on Saturday and Sunday night. She was excited because the minister thought it was possible. In addition, she shared about how we visit in homes to encourage families and give them hope for their home, whatever their situation.

She was on the phone with the minister off and on throughout the day while I kept walking. At one point, she told me the minister had talked with the deacons and was excited and optimistic about our being able to park our RV on their property, and he thought he might have a family for us to visit. He told Glenda that he wanted to talk with me.

On my break from walking that afternoon, the minister, Damian Phillips, called and we talked. It was exciting. He confirmed that the deacons said we could park on their property, plus he did have a family for us to visit. Glenda was amazing. Getting a visit through a minister for a family with a "man walking across America" is not an easy task. Without a "referral," most ministers are wisely protective of their flock or church family. Damian

Phillips checked out our website and references. He had gone the extra mile in inviting us for the weekend.

Before the phone call ended and I got back to walking, Pastor Phillips said, "Oh, and yes, the deacons said you can preach this Sunday."

I was shocked and assured him that we had not asked to preach. I knew that was pushing it. He then asked if I had a sermon I could preach about the *Walk*. I assured him I had three sermons that I could preach. He then said that I could preach one of them and asked if I would like to preach in both morning services. WOW! It was getting better by the moment—a place for the RV, a family to visit, and preaching in two services. Glenda (and the Lord) had just hit a grand slam. Damian and I agreed on all three and said goodbye. I hugged Glenda, and with excitement racing through my body; I was walking again, much faster than before.

We didn't know it then, but our stop at Canton, Kentucky, would be one of the highlights of the Walk for many reasons. Looking back, we can see God's hand-prints all over this stop in Canton.

BGEA Team

On Saturday, July 20, the same BGEA Team (David Lamar, Ron, and Jason) met us at 6:00 a.m. in Farmington, Kentucky, to film me getting ready for the day. It was awesome to start the day with them. They expressed their amazement at the details that I went through in getting prepared for walking for a full day. They had no idea that there was that much to do every morning. (See Appendix D for Jim's Daily Morning Prep for Walking.) They filmed throughout the day as I walked and as Glenda drove.

Glenda's Glimpses: Catching Him in Action?

We finally reached Hwy 80 and it turned out to be a wonderful divided highway with wide shoulders and lighter traffic. I could see Jim easily and my spirit could relax a bit. The video team had looked forward to taping out here in a country setting to meet the people with whom Jim made contact. They had heard some of the stories about his encountering people along the road, stopping to talk to Jim, and they were looking forward to "catching him in action." Well, it didn't happen. It was an unusually quiet day.

Many times people would pull over and talk to Jim. Actually, I talked to many officers and a few Department of Transportation people. They would pull over where I was parked and ask if I was okay and if I needed help. When I would explain what Jim was doing, they would invariably say something like, "Really?" and off we would go into a conversation. It was fun. I even had one officer look at a map to help me know what would be the best route to go.

The video team was looking forward to taping such things, but no one, I mean no one, pulled over to talk to either one of us while they were there. Thinking back, when people saw the video team, they might have decided that they didn't want to be on film.

God's Perfect Timing

On Sunday, July 21, the BGEA Team filmed us at the Canton Baptist Church where I preached in both services. In the afternoon, the team filmed a family visit with the Mitchell family, one of the highlight visits of the entire *Walk*. Following the filming of the Mitchell family, Glenda and I drove back to the church for the evening service and had one of the strongest rain storms of the *Walk* accompany us back to the church. Praise God I wasn't walking. It was hard enough driving in it, let alone trying to imagine how I would have walked in it. So many times on the *Walk*, it rained the hardest at night or on Sunday when I wasn't walking. Coincidence? Not a chance!

Special Family – Mitchell family

The Mitchell's are special friends in Jesus whom we met on the *Walk*! Their names are Greg, Melissa, Caleb, and Megan. Their family is one to remember. In fact, after the *Walk*, we have still been in touch with them. The interview was memorable. The BGEA Team videoed it and did separate interviews with Greg and Melissa.

After my sermon that morning, a young lady told me she connected with me as I shared in my message about how my mother died of a heart attack at age thirty-seven when I was ten. The young lady thanked me for sharing that, telling me that both of her parents had died.

We learned later that she was Megan, the niece of Greg Mitchell, whose brother (Megan's dad) died in a calf-roping accident three years earlier. Her dad had been raising her since her mother was killed in a car accident when Megan was five. Megan was also in that accident. She now lives with her Uncle Greg and family.

We met Greg at church. He was a man in a wheelchair, but very mobile, going everywhere with an exuberant spirit that was touching. He was excited that we were coming to their home in the afternoon for a visit and an interview. He was eager to meet with us.

Melissa, wife and mom, said she was shy and seemed to think she would be intimidated by the video cameras. She wasn't. It was a testimony to the professionalism of the BGEA Team and the focus of the interview. Glenda and I visited and shared our desire for every home to have Jesus living in the home with the family. We shared for an hour about the joy and the hope that comes through Jesus living in our lives so He can live in the home.

Mitchell family

It was touching for Glenda and me to hear the stories of Greg's accident, confining him to the wheelchair as a paraplegic for life. We were moved by Megan's story of the deaths of her parents. Caleb was adopted and had been an only child until Megan moved in. He said it really changed his life in the family, but said he was adapting to the change. Melissa was refreshing, being honest about how difficult things had been, but never losing hope because Jesus was with them.

We prayed at the close of the interview, which included sharing our excitement about Dr. Billy Graham's message of "Hope America" coming in November of 2013. During the personal interviews, Greg and Melissa shared more about their hope that comes from Jesus in their lives.

This was and is an impressive family who became a special family for us that helped make the stop in Canton a highlight of the *Walk.*

Glenda's Glimpses: Powerful Sermon

Sunday, July 21, was a memorable day. Jim's preaching was powerful. He really spoke mightily about his passion and the message God had assigned him. I was so proud of him, and at the same time, humbled by how God was putting things together.

After going to dinner with some church people, we spent the afternoon at the Mitchell's home. Greg Mitchell was amazing. He didn't let his physical challenges stop him. He had done a lot of building in their house, but even greater, neither he nor his sweet wife, Melissa, allowed it to stop them in their home life. There were so many dynamics going on within the family. They were determined to show their niece, Megan, that life can still be good although both her mom and dad had died. Then there was the challenge for them to help their son, Caleb, be able to adapt from being an only child to welcoming someone who needed a lot of comfort. Caleb was willing to share what that was like for him. The family was a shining light for what it means to have Jesus in the home.

REFLECTIONS ON WEEK 16

Looking back, we can see God's handprints all over this stop in Canton.

So many times on the Walk, it rained the hardest at night or on Sunday when I wasn't walking. Coincidence? Not a chance!

The Buckley family is far from perfect. Life has not been easy. We have faced death, serious illnesses and challenging struggles, but our family has Jesus walking with us through all the battles, claiming victory ultimately in Him.

****

Love the LORD your God with all your heart and with all your soul and with all your strength. These commandments that I give you today are to be upon your hearts. Impress them on your children. (Deuteronomy 6:5-7a)

Week 17

July 22-28 – Canton, KY to Glasgow, KY

141.6 Miles

My Old Kentucky Home

A Beautiful Morning Walk

E arly Monday morning, I walked on a quiet lane beside a beautiful lake. This was a gorgeous walk, compliments of Glenda and her iPad. Glenda was pleased with herself for finding this road. Her trusty iPad had become a very important companion. The road was the old Hwy 68. We saw only a couple of cars on such a pretty stretch of the road, and it actually saved a couple miles!

Beautiful little lake

While in Canton, Kentucky, the rain almost drowned us on Sunday night. It rained hard from 3:00 a.m. on, with lightning and thunder, but not with the winds that we've had before that tossed the RV back and forth. It was just a lot of water. Some even came in through the one window we normally had open because the rain came at such an angle.

I felt the humidity as I walked on Monday, even though it was cooler. Rain threatened us all day, but never came, so I kept walking.

My physical body was completely drained. After such a full day Sunday, I felt flat, but had a good time praying with the Lord. This was one of those days that I felt like He was carrying me all day, as I was completely wiped out.

I think being used by the Lord completely exhausted me. The church had over 100 people in the first service with a little less in the second service. The people received well the Lord's message that I had the privilege of delivering.

The message was about Jesus impacting our homes, our nation, and our world, one life, and one home at a time. I stated in the sermon that if each person would make the decision to have Him as the one who lives in our hearts and our homes, then the world could change.

A Surprise Blessing!

When I preached in Canton, Dr. Mike Rust, director of the Little River Baptist Association, was present and offered us a "surprise blessing." It was a place to stay on Monday, July 22, at the Little River Baptist Association's guest housing.

What a treat. For one night, we had a nicely furnished bedroom and use of the kitchen, washer and dryer, and a lovely bathroom equipped with a tub. Wow! We took advantage of his gracious gift doing laundry, having a nice dinner, and even watching the news on television, something we had not done on the *Walk*.

Thank you, Dr. Rust, and thanks to the Lord for providing another surprise blessing on the *Walk*. We left on Tuesday, July 23, fully appreciating how great our Lord is, but also how many great people "hidden in America" are blessing lives every day. The news media doesn't cover enough of the "good news" from good people, but we saw it, received it, and were blessed by it. Our news media seems to specialize in the "big" while ignoring the "little." What we enjoyed were little towns in America. They need to be featured. I know the media is in the big cities, but they need to venture out more and cover the people and the places that keep America strong. The little towns are full of solid, sound, and committed Americans.

We rested in one of those "small, out-of-the-way places" that night. It was awesome!

Glenda's Glimpses: "Spreading Out" a Little

It was nice to "spread out" a little bit. We had access to more than our usual floor space of 2 ½ by 8 feet in the motorhome. I didn't have to wait in one spot until Jim was finished with whatever before I could walk to the other end of the motorhome (all eight feet). I wear a pedometer all the time, and it won't register steps unless I have walked so many steps at a time. I could clean the whole motorhome registering very few steps. I realized towards the end of the *Walk* that I had cabin fever. I typically spent twenty to twenty-two hours a day inside the motorhome. A "spreading out" oasis was nice.

Amish Hospitality after WKDZ Interview

After a comfortable stay at the Little River Baptist Association guest housing, I walked about five miles before meeting Glenda in Cadiz, Kentucky, for an interview on the "Alan & Alan" show. It was brief (about ten minutes), but so much fun sharing the story of the *Walk* with people in Kentucky.

Our kids picked up the station on internet, and being great kids, they thought we were terrific. One even suggested that we should have our own talk show. That was nice, but walking was our mission – I walked twenty-three plus miles that day. We ended the day shopping at an Amish store located in Fairview, Kentucky, and dry camping near the barn and shed of an Amish family with seven children.

I asked Steve, the Amish father of seven, about dry camping at the Jefferson Davis Memorial near his home. He said he didn't think camping was allowed there. However, he said we could park in his yard and spend the night safely in our RV on his property. We accepted and thanked him.

He declined posing for a picture, but did say if we "happened to catch them in a photograph," that was up to us. Glenda tried getting photos of his kids racing bikes around the barn, but could never get a good shot. They were fast and were a blur in every attempt. She had fun trying. The day was long, but started well and ended well, thanks to Amish hospitality.

Glenda's Glimpses: Whizzing Bikes

Although the kids weren't allowed to pose, I think they were hoping to "get caught" with a snapshot. They just kept whizzing by while I was trying to fix dinner in the motorhome. Every time I would hear them coming, I would hurry to the door to try to catch them in a photo, but I was always too slow.

The Amish, Glenda, and a Load of Melons

This morning was committed to the Amish. I saw an Amish lady with a little girl in a nice cart going down the road. I got three pictures of them. As they passed me, the lady gave a little wave of thank you.

Young Amish farmer

Then I saw four big horses pulling a cart ahead of me on the other side of the road, so I called Glenda. It was on her side. She drove past them to get a picture as they came by. She pulled off the road and the driver stopped. They talked for at least twenty minutes before I arrived. She loved meeting people and visiting with them. It's part of the life of this marvelous woman.

Glenda's Glimpses: Not of This World

I asked the young man driving the horses if he would mind if I took a picture, and he said that it would be fine. I learned that he belonged to the same group of Amish of the family where we stayed. Each Amish/Mennonite group has their own set of "standards."

Back at the auction yard, we first started getting glimpses of the Amish and Mennonite people. While parked in the auction yard, we saw an Amish gentleman driving a tractor pulling a covered, box trailer in front of the auction yard. He stopped, and out climbed his wife and children from the trailer. This group had decided they could have tractors to work the hard soil.

Some groups use only animals for pulling plows and other equipment, some are allowed to have a tractor, some men and boys wear overalls and a hat, some wear suspenders. The women wear dresses and nets in their hair over their bun. Their whole premise is that while they are *in* the world, they are not to be *of* the world.

This young man said he had an eighth-grade education as did all the men. They are very committed to their standards, and all of those we met were very friendly. I even drove back ten miles once to have a wonderful Mennonite woman sign my memory quilt. We had been interviewed by her and her husband the night before for their national paper. We had so much fun. After signing the quilt, she gave me some homemade bread and jam to take with me. Later on the trip, she called me to see how we were doing.

Jim: I caught up with Glenda as she was talking, and met Jonas, the driver. At twenty-six, he was getting married very soon. He had four strong work horses, pulling two trailers of melons. He talked to Glenda for quite a while. I got pictures of him and Glenda, and then pictures of the horses and found out that he was Mennonite, not Amish. He wore suspenders, and was somewhat clean shaven. Glenda met his cousin later on the road. She was twenty-three, and shared with Glenda that Amish in their group have to marry in their community; they can't marry outside, which is fascinating. Glenda took her picture.

We had an interesting morning with the Amish and Mennonites.

What a Family!

On July 26, as we walked through Bowling Green, Kentucky, we went to the home of a family referred to us by David Wright, Vice President of TCM. David so highly regarded this family that he wanted us to meet them and share the story of the *Walk* with them.

Late in the afternoon, we arrived at the home of Thad and Tammy Crews. On a memorable night, we enjoyed some magnificent people. Thad, a professor of business communications at Western Kentucky University and a supporter of TCM, was very interested in missions and what I do as an adjunct professor for TCM International Institute. As David had suggested, Thad was also very interested in the *Walk*, asking many questions. I had a fascinating discussion with him, a brilliant man.

Tammy, a lovely mother of three teenagers, cares for the family and supports her husband, and creates a lovely home atmosphere, even though she has muscular dystrophy. It was beautiful to see how the family works together to make the home such a warm and welcoming place. We could have visited all night, but we finally had to check on the computer "stuff" and get to bed. We got to bed late again, but spending time with this family was worth it.

Glenda's Glimpses: Bouncing "Bible" Kids

I passed Jim and was looking for a good place to park for a while to watch for him to come, in our usual "leap-frog" style. I just settled on my next parking spot when I looked across this two-lane road and decided I could more easily see Jim coming, parked on the other side. I was going to have to park behind a car parked in my "usual" parking spot. I had not noticed before, but that car had little heads excitedly sticking out of the windows. Pretty soon a man and four bouncing kids did just that–bounced out of and around the car.

Then I heard them say, "Here he comes!" Being very perceptive, I realized they were waiting for Jim. I went to talk to them, and sure enough, that's exactly what they were doing. They had passed him on the road and saw his bright orange shirt that said, "I'M WALKING ACROSS AMERICA." They wanted to meet "the man."

When Jim came up, we chatted with them. The man's name was Paul with four children named Peter, James, John, and Moriah. Those are four "Bible names" as Peter, James, and John went with Jesus up on a mountain where He was transfigured and where Moses and Elijah joined them. Mount Moriah was a mountain where many important things happened including Solomon building the temple. We had a great conversation with this family learning about family heartaches they had been through. We encouraged them, then prayed with them.

A Great Sunday in Glasgow, Kentucky

We met the minister, Richard Martin, and his wife, Patty. Richard gave me an opportunity to share in the service by interviewing me. If people didn't know, the interview would have convinced them that Richard and I were well-acquainted and pre-planned the interview. During the interview when I was responding, he laughed because my answer was his next question. We connected so well, even though we had just met minutes before the service.

Interview in Glasgow

Without our "pre-planning this," Richard's message was about the heart of our message on the *Walk*. His sermon was built around the question, "Are you the real deal?" He emphasized dropping all facades in our lives and being real with people. With Jesus living in our homes, that's what we do—we drop facades and become real. We thought it was a terrific connection to the *Walk*, without preplanning it.

Again, we saw God at work. It was His Walk.

Glenda's Glimpses: Caring Churches

I had been able to reach Pastor Martin by email to ask if we could stay in the parking lot. He had sent back an email saying it would be fine. Whenever I would contact someone from a church, I would tell them about our website. Richard had apparently looked up the website and had done some research on us. When we met him Sunday morning, he was so welcoming. We stayed there again that night, and they left the church unlocked for us to be able to go in and out if we needed. Actually, several churches did that across the country.

We were well cared for by so many churches.

I really enjoyed the service. Right in front of us was a toddler who sat on his dad's shoulders during the praise time. I've never seen so much energy during the singing. He just bounced like crazy with the music. I wouldn't be surprised if the dad's shoulders were sore.

Kentucky: My Roots!

Kentucky was home for my Grandad Buckley, who came from Waddy, Kentucky, to California a long time ago (100 years). As I walked through Kentucky for several days, I had the strange feeling that I was "home." At least I was walking on land from where the roots for the Buckley side of my family came.

It was fun walking, thinking, praying, rejoicing, and reflecting on Grandad Bevley (B) Buckley, whom I knew as a hardworking farmer and a man of deep faith in God. He was a very strong man about whom there are legends of his physical strength. I possess an old photo of Grandad Buckley harvesting grain, driving a team of mules pulling a huge harvester. In the picture, the driver is perched on a precarious seat. Handwritten on the back of the photo, the caption reads:

Bevley Buckley
21146 Avenue 21
Madera, California

Taken about 1914
Harvester drawn by 36 head of mules.

On one of the rounds harvesting, the driver's seat broke and Mr. Buckley called the lead team's names to stop. They obeyed at once. He walked out unhurt. It was his lucky day.

That was my Grandad Buckley in California, but his roots were in the land in which I was now walking where he learned how to walk, physically and spiritually. He always walked with Jesus, and I am seeking to follow in his steps. I pray my grandchildren will seek to follow in my steps of faith. In a sense, this *Walk* book is a tribute to my grandad. That tribute is partially rooted in the spelling of the word, "Grandad." In some dictionaries, there are two spellings. Granddad with two "ds" is the preferred American spelling. The British preferred spelling is with one "d." Though my grandad was not British, he spelled his grandad with one "d" as did my dad. So I do, also.

Does that make us British or just different? My grandad would say "special," and he was. Praise God, I was able to walk through his roots in Kentucky, a special place to me.

Why Walk?

Yesterday, a newspaper reporter asked me why I chose to walk across America to emphasize my cause. He was asking why I didn't choose something more productive. I thought about that as I walked and came up with the following response.

I believe I was called by God to walk across America. I walked to convey a message of hope for the homes and hearts of America. Yes, I could have written a book, but it seemed premature because it seemed like I needed to earn a hearing to convey the message.

In best-selling author Michael Hyatt's, *Platform: Get Noticed in a Noisy World,* he emphasizes that there are five steps to guide anyone with something to say or sell. Step One: Start with Wow! He describes "Wow... as a transcendent moment... that has some combination... of ten elements." As I reflected after the *Walk,* I was surprised how many of the ten elements applied to the *Walk.* The *Walk* was the WOW! Hyatt closes out his ten elements on pages 8-10 with the statement that the WOW "is the foundation to building a significant platform."

Based on Hyatt's book, the *Walk* was a great way to start building a platform to get the message out. The *Walk* was building a platform. Was the *Walk* a WOW? Based on the response before, during, and after the *Walk,* having a sixty-six-year-old pastor, husband, father, and grandfather walking across America in six months, averaging over twenty-two miles a day captured the attention of people. I was walking out of obedience to God. However, in His wisdom, I was creating a platform for the message of hope for the homes and hearts of America by walking. That hope was Jesus living in every home.[2]

---

[2] Michael Hyatt, *Platform: Get Noticed in a Noisy World,* Thomas Nelson, Nashville, Tennessee. 2012.

WOW! I was building a platform for God's message of hope through Jesus to be heard by the entire nation. I didn't even know that at the time. The message for me and you is to trust God and do what He tells us to do! He knows what He is doing and calling us to do, even if we don't know it all at the time.

Simple obedience is highly underrated.

In addition to creating a platform, I was also learning so much while walking. About half way across America, I reflected on the *Walk*–how similar this *Walk* was to raising a family, something Glenda and I have been working on for over forty years. We had invested heavily in this *Walk*, but we invested more heavily in raising our family.

My mind began to race as I recorded in my recorder thoughts comparing the *Walk* to raising a family. I had so much to say that when transcribed, I had over 3,000 words, longer than most weekly stories of the *Walk*. I had the makings of another book. I wondered to myself, how many people have done both–walked across America and spent over forty years raising a family? I don't know, but I know one who has.

After much thought, my final answer to the reporter's question is that I was walking out of obedience to God, but that walking was proving to be the best way for me to promote the cause of Jesus living in every home.

He called me to walk, so I did. I learned so much and am still learning.

REFLECTIONS ON WEEK 17

The Walk was not my idea. It was God's idea. He called me to walk, so I did.

WOW! What an awesome God we serve!

The home is the place where faith blossoms, grows deep, and produces changes. We are beginning to see how the Walk built a platform for that message to continue after the Walk.

****

I am reminded of your sincere faith, a faith that dwelt first in your grandmother Lois and your mother Eunice and now, I am sure, dwells in you as well. (2 Timothy 1:5 ESV)

Week 18

July 29 - August 4 – Glasgow, KY to Barbourville, K Y
150 Miles

Kentucky Gets Exciting

Telling the Story in Columbia, Kentucky

On July 29, I began walking at 6:45 a.m. on the 120th day of the *Walk across America.* We picked up where we left off about four miles outside of Edmonton after having a very wonderful time with the people at Glenview Christian Church in Glasgow, Kentucky, yesterday. Monday morning I was sluggish from the lack of sleep the last two nights, so I stopped and took a midmorning twenty-minute nap. That helped, but it didn't rejuvenate me like I had hoped. I didn't wake up with a spark, and four hours into the morning, I had walked only six miles, which was dreadfully slow.

During the day, Glenda had arranged with the minister of the Columbia Christian Church, Terry White, for us to camp in the church parking lot with access to water and electricity. Super!

Very late that day, I walked into Columbia, a small town, established in 1802. I was exhausted, but thankful that I was close to my daily goal of twenty-five miles. When I arrived at the church, Terry had set up an appointment with a young reporter of the local newspaper who took copious notes for an article for their weekly newspaper.

In talking with him, I learned that he was also the sports editor and the editor of the paper. He told me that the editor passed away last year, so he was taking over the paper. I liked him.

He asked me a very interesting question, "What is the hardest thing for you about the *Walk*?"

Without thinking, I said, "Tomorrow."

He said, "Wow!"

It was not only a good answer, but the right answer. Yes, after walking twenty-five miles that day, I will do it again tomorrow and the next day. Exhausted and relaxed, "tomorrow" just popped out when he asked the question. Praise God for Columbia, another special small town in America.

After the interview, Terry and his wife, Marci, took Glenda and me to dinner. We enjoyed the meal and our time with them. Terry invited us to come back on Wednesday night for his seniors' Bible study and share the *Walk* story. We did and were thrilled to tell the story to over fifty people about our *Walk* across America, inviting people to have Jesus in their hearts and homes. Terry has been the minister in Columbia Christian Church for twenty-six years and is doing a great job of touching hearts and homes for Jesus.

During dinner, we learned that Terry and Marci know Richard Martin very well, the minister in the town we just left. We were amazed at the connections in these small, but very important towns across America.

Columbia was a good stop for us. It was refreshing after a long day.

Glenda's Glimpses: Small Towns Meet Needs

Although many times I wasn't able to reach anyone in the office of these churches, I was fortunate to reach someone two days in a row—first in Glasgow, and then in Columbia, Kentucky. Terry White, the minister at the Columbia Christian Church, not only connected the motorhome to electricity and water, but he left a door ajar at the church so we could go in. That was nice because there was a bathroom with a shower right off the gymnasium. We enjoyed having dinner with Terry and Marci at a local café. Getting to know others in ministry has been a real joy for us. There are so many we would like to see again this side of heaven.

The town was actually not the easiest place to maneuver around in a motorhome. I had become much braver and even a bit more skillful, even if I do say so myself. I needed to find a place to get the oil changed. I found a small automotive shop. They didn't have room to do it inside the garage, so I had to use some of my skill to drive the nose down an incline under the eaves of the garage. I didn't feel really secure about their skills, but they did very well. Boy, we truly were seeing small town America. Columbia was a quaint town with a feel of history.

To Walk or Not to Walk? That Is the Question!

Walking on parkways in Kentucky was in question. A parkway can look like an interstate highway, but it is not legally called one. I could not walk on interstate highways. We knew that. When we asked authorities if we could walk on parkways, some states said "yes" and some said "no." In Kentucky, we were getting different answers.

Glenda was stopped by a state trooper, but he approved us being on the parkway. Later, a different officer stopped me and said that I couldn't walk on the parkways. His name was Brian, a really nice deputy sheriff. I explained that we were approved by a state trooper. Before that state trooper agreed to let me keep walking, he had asked me if I was raising money. I told him that we're not raising money, but we're raising the hopes of the American home. We believe that they can have help in their home by having the difference maker live in their home and that is Jesus. He agreed and said my cause was good, but be careful out there. I assured him that we were being very careful and loved the parkway's wide shoulder. Brian was satisfied and let me continue walking.

A Department of Transportation (DOT) gentleman came the same day to Glenda, and he reluctantly approved it after Glenda talked to him for a while. She's very persuasive.

Glenda's Glimpses: Pepper Spray Ready

This DOT supervisor really startled me. I didn't see him come up. He came on the passenger side and banged on the side of the motorhome. I should have been getting used to that because that's what many of the officers would do. I know I'm a pretty dangerous character, but this time it startled me, maybe because it was on the other side and I didn't see him in the side-view mirror. I opened the window a little and had my pepper spray in hand. He was a bit gruff at first, but as I talked, he became more amiable. I told him about our website and Facebook page. I noticed that night that he had "liked" us on Facebook. In fact, "Jim" followed us the rest of the trip on Facebook, and commented when we finished the *Walk*. After he left me, he drove on down the road, turned around and came back the other way by "my" Jim and honked and waved big. Jim had no idea who he was and why he waved at him as if he were waving to a good friend.

Excerpt from the Road: "Dad's Been Arrested?"

A different kind of a day. It is now 6:42 p.m. and I'm still walking. I would have been done by now, but a sheriff's supervisor stopped me on the parkway and overrode what others had said was okay. Three Department of Transportation guys, a previous sheriff's deputy, and two state troopers all had said we could walk on the parkway.

I reasoned with him that walking on some of the other roads with no shoulder on a country road is far more dangerous than walking on the parkway – with twelve foot shoulders plus another five feet off the side of the road. It's like a seventeen-foot shoulder that I can get to very quickly. I'm walking into traffic – I can see approaching vehicles. He said the parkway was too dangerous. People are going eighty miles an hour.

Again, nicely, I said that they go fast on the country roads, too. Bowing his head, he agreed reluctantly. He knew what I was saying, but the problem was that people had called in to the Sheriff's station about "an old man walking with a cane" on the parkway.

I told him that I'm only sixty-six. I'm young. He smiled. And with a cane? It was a walking stick. It's a big difference.

He took me in his sheriff's car because he wouldn't let me walk anymore anywhere. He was as nice as he could be, and we developed a quick friendship of sorts. When we arrived at our RV, he met Glenda and left with good spirit, but it was disappointing to have to find a country road. We reluctantly found one.

That country road was un-walkable, so I've been walking around town to bank miles to finish the day. I've got about a mile and a half to go. So, that's my situation. It's starting to sprinkle a little. Glad I have an umbrella just in case it sprinkles a lot.

(Later) The RV is all hooked up with water and electricity at a church in Russell Springs, Kentucky.

My brother, Tom, called today to see how I was doing and at the end of the call said, "Be careful." Timely.

We'll stay here tonight, walk more miles tomorrow somewhere.

It will be to God's glory, and we're going to get across the nation one way or another.

Glenda's Glimpses: "Do it again!"

I was waiting for Jim and thought it was taking a while, then looked back and saw a trooper's car with flashing lights. I started to worry, then I saw Jim standing by the car, talking to the officer. Pretty soon Jim got in and they turned around and came towards me. By then I had texted all the kids, and their texts were flying back.

About the time Jim and the officer were walking around the RV, the kids said, "Did you get a picture?"

I was a little flustered and didn't so they said, "Have Dad do it again!"

"What, and get him arrested this time?" I asked the officer if I could get a picture of him and he declined.

Oh well, it just has to be etched in my mind.

Jim decided to walk down to a little town just south of Russell Springs because I found a laundromat down there. It was just across the street from a Christian Church. After I finished the laundry, I went into the church office and had a chance to visit with two of the ladies. One of them was a young wife and mother that shared with me both some challenges within her home life and also some encouraging things that were happening. We prayed together. She has a soft spot in my heart. I still get their church newsletters by email.

Jim Meets Jim

Tuesday, July 30, in the morning, I was stopped by Jim, a stone mason driving from Beattyville to Bowling Green to do a masonry repair job. He was a red-headed, red-bearded guy, probably in his early forties who looked like a rugged mountain man. However, he had a soft heart. We talked over half an hour about faith, Jesus living in homes and in lives. He was intrigued with that.

Jim talks with Jim

Living in Eastern Kentucky, he described where he lived as a place accented by prescription drug problems. He went back in history to the Harlan County Wars several years ago. He was just a fascinating man whom I connected with immediately. He was captured by the idea of faith, especially when I told him about cowboy churches.

When he asked me what was the craziest thing that I'd seen on the *Walk*, I was stumped. Glenda came over to take pictures. Having Glenda join me on this adventure also fascinated him. Later, when I told him I thought the craziest thing I'd seen was an old guy like me walking across America, he laughed.

I told him one of the cutest things I had seen was my wife falling in love with a turtle, and having the turtle for over a month in the RV. He loved that story.

After he left, I was rejuvenated. It was amazing. I felt better as I was walking with a bounce in my step, maybe even picking up some miles that I'd lost during the stop.

It pays to slow down and spend time with people. God must have been pleased enough to help me make up the time.

Glenda's Glimpses: Jim Connects

This is another picture that will be etched in my mind, but this one I did get on "film." Jim was slow coming as I was ahead of him. I was parked, as I was so often, on the opposite side of a divided highway. In that area of the country, they had what were called "crossovers." It was a service road that would go from one side of the divided highway to the other. They were designed for making U-turns instead of their having to build an overpass. They didn't go anywhere except to the other side. I really liked them because there were times I couldn't see Jim for a stretch and so I would go back and check on him. That's one of the reasons I drove 9,000 miles. Anyway, I looked back and there was Jim, talking away. The guy was leaning up against his blue car, fully engaged. Jim has such a way of being able to connect with people quickly. I saw it many times.

Walking in the Fog

Early in the morning, I was walking east in Kentucky in the fog. We were now in the Eastern Time Zone. As I walked that morning, I couldn't see the sun, but visibility was good for driving purposes. Drivers could see at least three hundred yards ahead. We declared it safe for walking.

We ended up spending the previous night at Ott's General Store/ Service Station near London, Kentucky. Some Good Ole Boys were sitting in rocking chairs out in front of the store when we arrived that afternoon. Mr. James R. Boggs, the owner, treated us to dinner of chicken strips and potato wedges. I sat with the Good Ole Boys, rocking with them for a short time. Kind of nice. Glenda and I camped there in the parking lot that night.

Mr. Boggs, head of the Good Ole Boys, was a helpful and interesting man who said he serviced the whole area: farmers, hunters, fishermen, marijuana growers, and moonshiners. He even called the London paper and alerted them to me walking across America. That call led to a phone interview, a picture, and an excellent article in the London paper. Later, the paper was given to me by a gentleman who looked for and found me on the *Walk*.

Glenda's Glimpses: Packin' Man

I have to talk about the Good Ole Boys. We were able to get a good picture of them rocking in their chairs in front of the general store. As I was getting ready to leave, I told Mr. Boggs how I have found the people to be so nice around there.

Hangin' out with the Good Ole Boys

He said, "Oh, they are when they know you have one of these" as he lifted a small revolver out of his shirt pocket.

I hadn't hugged a "packin' man" before. It's a different world from ours, but seems to work for them. (Later in a phone conversation, Mr. Boggs reassured me that he was licensed to carry a concealed weapon.) The Good Ole Boys were a fun group and we enjoyed our stop.

REFLECTIONS ON WEEK 18

*It seems that Jesus was having a good time introducing us to a new culture
that is full of very interesting and fun people.
His creativity blossomed with a variety of "new friends."*

****

*Jesus said to him, "Today salvation has come to this house, because this man,
too, is a son of Abraham. For the Son of Man came to seek and to save what
was lost."*
(Luke 19:9-10)

Week 19

August 5-11 – Barbourville, KY to Bristol, VA
140 Miles

Lots of States and Things

Share about the Walk? Absolutely!

A fresh *Walk* week began at 6:50 a.m. on August 5, entering week nineteen. Leaving Barbourville, Kentucky, we saw signs that stated that this was the home of the first battle in Kentucky during the Civil War–a battle of the Confederates attacking the Union soldiers and destroying a Union soldiers' training camp. The Confederates were repelled twice until they attacked from a different direction and pushed the Union soldiers back. They were evidently fighting in open fields, shooting at each other as they were lined up–that resulted in fifteen of the Union soldiers being killed and four or five of the Confederate soldiers. The town also claimed to be Daniel Boone's home town or at least where he lived. Some people said he lived lots of places.

The morning was cool and foggy compared to the much warmer weather that we had been facing. Even with the fog, visibility for walking was good. Also, I walked in town for over an hour which made it safe to walk in foggy weather. With a town of about 3,000 people, it looked like it would have a bigger population, but we learned that townships were really small in that area because they don't include the county population. Barbourville serviced many more thousands that lived outside of town. It was big enough to have a Walmart, and we learned that a Walmart will often be in the towns that are centers for people.

Yesterday, we had a great time at the First Baptist Church in Barbourville. We didn't know anybody; we didn't even RV camp in their parking lot. We just went to church. We were greeted by two deacons at the door, and we gave them our *invitingAmericahome.org* cards and shared quickly what we were doing. They took us to an adult class where we were welcomed after we were introduced via the card. Before going to class, we met the pastor, Shane Nickell, and when I gave him a card, he said, "I recognize you." Evidently, he had seen something on TV news or Facebook.

After Sunday school, Pastor Nickell asked me if I would take ten minutes in the service to share about the *Walk* and give my testimony. "Absolutely!" That went well, and after the service he had us stand at the door by him. Everybody that came through wanted a card with our web site on it, so that was exciting.

We went to lunch with a couple who were fascinated with our journey. We talked about ministry, life, and family. It was good. We went back to the RV and took a big nap, did a lot of stuff on the computer, and rested.

I started walking Monday morning with either hay fever or a head cold. I didn't know which one, but it didn't matter. I was walking; that's what mattered.

Walmart Truck Driver

Midmorning on August 6, I had already walked for an hour to join Glenda for a delicious Cracker Barrel breakfast and was walking toward Cumberland Gap tunnel. As I walked across a parking lot, a Walmart truck driver walked toward me with something in his hand.

> *He said he was glad to finally see me when he was*
> *stopped because he had been watching me walk for*
> *over 200 miles and wondered why I was walking*
> *across America.*

He held in his hand a newspaper from London, Kentucky, that answered his question. He was excited to hear that I was walking for Jesus to be in every home in America. Mr. Boggs, of the Good Ole Boys, had prompted the newspaper article.

The truck driver, John, said he was inspired by the *Walk*. Humbled, I thanked him for the encouraging words and the newspaper that he gave me as a gift. After he took a picture of us on his cell phone, I departed with a lift in my step. I was thankful to John for seeing me on the *Walk*, finding out "why" I was walking, then finding me and thanking me for walking. When he told me I was his "inspiration," I left feeling the same about him. He was an inspiration to me.

Cracker Barrel breakfast, a Walmart truck driver, and now on to Cumberland Gap. What a day! August 6 was becoming a very memorable day; it wasn't even noon, yet.

Times Square Church – New York City

I made contact with Times Square Church today. I called to let them know we're coming and ending our *Walk* in Times Square, only a few blocks from the church. I told them we didn't expect them to do anything, but just letting them know that we will be ending the Jesus *Walk* near them. The lady on the phone made note of our *Walk* and thanked me for calling.

Non-walkable Tunnel?

> *Having walked over 2,000 miles confronted us with various obstacles which forced us to be creative, persistent, and careful.*

On August 6, we had an obstacle when we reached historic Cumberland Gap. Wikipedia says, "It is a pass through the Cumberland Mountains, a long ridge within the Appalachian Mountains near the junction of the states of Tennessee, Kentucky, and Virginia." The Government's National Park Service adds, "Cumberland Gap, the first great gateway to the west: the buffalo, the Native American, the long hunter, yes the pioneer... all traveled this route through the mountains into the wilderness of Kentucky."

As we approached Cumberland Gap with all its history, we were excited until we discovered that it had a tunnel taking traffic through the Appalachians. I was eager to walk through the mile-long tunnel until I discovered our obstacle. **There is no walking in the tunnel.** How does one walk across America when not allowed to walk? We asked the National Park officials who served/worked at the information center. They said that there was a hiking trail "around the tunnel."

That sounded like a simple solution, but it didn't turn out to be that simple.

First, the tunnel was one mile while the trail was three miles. I could walk that.

Second, the "trail" was not a simple walk. Had I not been in good shape and equipped with my walking sticks, I would have been in trouble. I was okay and could walk it, carefully.

Third, Glenda drove to meet me on the trail, then left the RV in the parking lot. We walked together which was fun, with Glenda intending to only walk to a certain point, then go back to get the RV. The "point" was on the map, but we walked and walked. We were confused because the "point" was a long way into the trail.

We actually ended up walking all the way to the other end of the trail. Then we had a bigger problem. How to get to the RV? I wouldn't let Glenda walk back alone, so we were both going to walk all the way back, doubling the distance of the trail, no longer simple.

As we pondered our dilemma, two state utility workers stopped at the "end of the trail" parking area for lunch. Overhearing our predicament, one man said he would eat, then drive Glenda back to the RV, which he did.

Thank you, Mr. State Worker. When Glenda returned with the RV, we ate, napped, and I walked on to Tennessee and Virginia, two states spaced minutes apart.

We'll never forget Cumberland Gap and the "non-walkable tunnel."

We faced each new obstacle with creativity, always remembering the day we walked in three states, went on an adventurous hike together, then depended on a great American to help us solve a complicated obstacle.

Glenda's Glimpses: Best Option

It all sounded so simple, but it was a bit frustrating and complicated. The workers didn't show up right away. I really hadn't intended on hiking all the way, though I have to admit it was a beautiful hike. What were we to do when we arrived at the park at the other end? There was a set of grandparents with their twin grandsons at the park, and we told them our predicament. They sympathized, but didn't offer any help. As we kept going over options, the workers arrived to have their lunch. What a blessing! I had a nice conversation with the young man who took me back to the RV, while Jim stayed with the other worker. Great Americans!

According to what I had discovered on maps and iPad, it seemed to be the best route to begin crossing the Appalachians. The Cumberland Gap Park dips down from Kentucky into Tennessee for only about a half mile then back up into Virginia. Jim got to add Tennessee to his list of states!

Finally, Some Buffalo

How could August 6 get any better? Cracker Barrel for breakfast. Walmart's truck driver for inspiration. Walking around the tunnel at Cumberland Gap. Walking in Kentucky, Tennessee, and Virginia in one day. What could top that? Buffalo.

I had expected to see buffalo on the plains of America in states like Oklahoma or Texas. Not one. In Virginia? Yes, at the close of the day, I saw two small herds of "large" buffalo as we entered Virginia. I was impressed. I walked over 2,000 miles to see them. They were worth the wait. Huge animals. Fenced in, but they didn't have to stay fenced in if they didn't want to. They chose to stay and enjoy the good life with food provided. Finally! I got to see some buffalo, landmarks of America, in Virginia.

Glenda's Glimpses: The Sound of Music

The next day as we headed through the mountains, I had stopped at a view site–beautiful! As Jim arrived for a short break, we met a mission group on their way to Kentucky to do some work at a church. After they left, Jim stood at the viewpoint with his arms out wide, overlooking the gorgeous valley and sang, "The hills are alive with the Sound of Music." That was fun! You see, we went to see *Sound of Music* on our first official date when we were eighteen and nineteen. The movie had just come out. We actually have had the opportunity to see those hills in Austria, where Jim teaches. It seems the movie on our first date, and our early dating walks were "prophetic" of things to come in our life together.

"The hills are alive..."

Glenda's Glimpses: Do You Have a Weapon?

That night we ended up in Saint Paul, Virginia. Places to park for the night weren't very promising. We saw an officer from the town parked, so we went to ask him. He told us we could go to the city park. When we got there, we drove to the back. It had a covered place for picnics, so we barbequed and had a picnic. It was a good thing it was covered because it began to rain.

We were parked between the picnic covering and the pretty little river. We were right where a trail took off and a couple runners/hikers came through. It was a pretty place. However, cars kept coming back there then leaving. It shook our confidence. Then a man came through, just finishing his walk with his dog while I was cleaning up the dishes. He said he was a coal miner, so he was expounding on his frustration over the Administration's hurting the coal mining industry and how it was going to put so many out of work. We talked about that, the *Walk*, then I asked him if he thought we would be safe there.

He said he thought so then asked, "You **are** carrying a weapon, aren't you?"

We decided maybe we'd better find another place. We ended up staying in the parking lot of a well-lit gas station.

Change in Plans

It was raining and Glenda needed to do laundry, so we went down to Bristol, Virginia. We spent the night in a Walmart on Saturday night just so Glenda could do laundry. We couldn't find laundromats easily on the Appalachian Trail nor in the Appalachian Mountains. At least they weren't listed on websites. We found one listed in Bristol, so we went there. It was off our path, but we believed it was God directing.

While driving to Bristol, we stopped for a moment on the side of the road for Glenda to fix some sandwiches. As she did that, my phone rang. A lady from Oregon was calling to interview me for an article she was writing in the quarterly bulletin of our college alma mater.

She was a good interviewer, asking excellent questions, probing deeper than many others had done. The interview was long enough to allow Glenda to finish making the sandwiches and for me to drive on, continuing the interview. I slowed at times to a standstill because the rain was pouring down on us so hard that it caused us to pull off the road. How long was the interview? I didn't time it, but it was at least an hour.

It was long enough that we reached Bristol during the interview, after which I ate my lunch. That was the day of the "longest drive to a laundromat" and the day of the "longest interview," but one of the best interviews. The result of the interview was the cover story for the Northwest Christian University's Bulletin for their Fall/Winter 2013 edition. That cover story opened the door to my speaking in the University Chapel on September 5, 2014, to a chapel full of people listening to the stories of the *Walk*.

Once in Bristol, we decided to go on to Elk Park, North Carolina, and worship on Sunday at the Heaton Christian Church where our son, Daniel, and his wife, Charity, had served. While living in Elk Park, their son Ryan died after being prematurely born as result of complications following Charity's burst appendix. Ryan is buried in Elk Park.

It was probably one of the biggest "God's timing things" on the Walk.

Glenda's Glimpses: We Remember Ryan

So many times rain waited until the end of the day. While Jim walked in rain before (rain without lightning), there was no walking this day. It was a huge downpour. Because of the downpour, we had to stop in a turnout to decide what to do. Because it had rained and because we had to drive a ways for a laundromat, and because the laundromat was located not far from where Daniel and Charity had ministered, it made it possible to go see our grandson Ryan's grave. If it hadn't rained so hard on a Saturday that close to Elk Park, it would never have happened. God worked it all out. We could never have planned it. God is so good.

We went to church that morning and saw people we knew through Daniel and Charity. After having dinner at the church, we went to a store, bought a pot of yellow mums, took them to Ryan's grave and planted them. We took pictures of each of us there at the graveside with the flowers. I later had twenty-five copies of the picture printed for each family member to carry across the bridge at the end of the *Walk*. Ryan was represented. **We remember Ryan.**

REFLECTIONS ON WEEK 19

It was probably one of the biggest "God's timing things" on the Walk.

We saw the Lord direct our paths so many times.

God worked it all out. We could never have planned it.

His timing is amazing.

God is so good!

****

Whether you turn to the right or to the left, your ears will hear a voice behind you, saying, "This is the way; walk in it." (Isaiah 30:21)

Week 20

August 12-18 – Bristol, VA to Salem, VA
128 Miles

Walking with Surprises

Good to See Friends

At 7:21 in the morning, August 12, another week of walking began. It was a new day after our special day on Sunday.

It was always good to see friends on the *Walk*, although we had discouraged people from joining me while I was walking. Highway walking seemed more dangerous than walking in cities. Plus, by this time in Virginia, we were a long way from the West Coast where most of our close contacts lived.

On August 13, the Atkinson/Emmon's family, very good friends, wanted to walk with me for part of a day. Originally from California, they had moved a few years ago to North Carolina. We told them to come join us for a few hours. (We bent one of our **Walk Rules**–See Appendix B –for the day, having people walk with me on the open road.)

It was great to see them (a young grandma, a mom, dad, and two children). It was not the best day for walking with a slight drizzle off and on, plus a very narrow shoulder, but we made the best of it, visiting as we walked.

I was very careful while they walked with me. The children, ages eight and twelve, were kept on the inside away from the road. In some spots I stopped and wouldn't let anyone walk with me due to the extra narrow shoulder.

Having fun, walking with friends

All in all, it was great to have them take the time, drive the distance, walk with me, and catch up on life.

Yes, it was very good to see friends on the Walk.

Curiosity Leads to Interview

On Wednesday, August 14, we walked in West Virginia for just a few miles. At noon, I met Glenda at a parking lot in a commercial area. Walking off the road toward the RV, I noticed a building with discs on top–I assumed it was a radio station.

I had lunch, short nap, foot rub, and was ready to walk. Walking from the parking lot to the road, I walked by the radio station and saw a design I couldn't make out from the distance. With my curiosity peaked, I walked closer and realized the design was a peacock–an NBC peacock. This was a television station, WVVA, with the call letters abbreviations for the two states, WV and VA. Clever.

Phoning Glenda, I told her I was going to go in and ask them to contact their NBC stations in New York to tell them that I was coming. It was intended to be tongue in cheek. Glenda joined me, and we walked in. We introduced ourselves and gave the lady at the front desk a flyer for the *Walk* to give to the station manager.

We started to leave when she said, "Wait a minute."

In a moment, a man came out and asked if we had time for an interview. I hated to delay the *Walk*, but for an interview, I had time.

It wasn't a long wait. A bright and energetic newscaster, Kayla Lambert, greeted us and wanted to interview us outside. First, she interviewed me, then Glenda. These were excellent interviews and aired in Bluefield that night. It was awesome. We met a young married newscaster who became a good friend in a few moments.

My curiosity led me to the peacock, which led us to an interview. I walked away with a bounce in my step. It was an exciting "pre-birthday" gift.

Glenda's Glimpses: Simply Proclaim It

From time to time, we would meet someone on the road or in a store who would say something like, "I read about you" or "I saw you on TV." We would often get caught off guard. Many times, we couldn't figure out what newspaper or station. We had a definite message to convey, and we will probably never know or need to know how far-reaching the message carried. Our part was to simply proclaim it, and trust God to do the rest.

Simple obedience is highly underrated!

Birthday Pancakes, August 15

Did I walk on my birthday? Absolutely. I was on a mission. Why stop because of a birthday? Instead, I celebrated turning sixty-seven by walking twenty-one miles. When Glenda asked me what I wanted for my birthday, I said, "Pancakes." She makes the best whole grain pancakes, but had been too busy to make them much on the *Walk*. (They are so good!)

In the evening, we celebrated with pancakes. I knew they were coming, so just the thought of the pancakes carried me all day. I was not disappointed. Yummy! Happy sixty-seven to me.

Glenda's Glimpses: Making Decisions

In 2010, Pearisburg, Virginia, had a population of 2,786. I'm sure most of you have never heard of it. We hadn't, but it played a very important part on the *Walk*. Why was it important?

As route planner, I had to figure out the best way to finish crossing the Appalachians. We had traveled up through a section earlier, but now we were at the threshold to the East Coast. We knew it wouldn't work where it was solid green on the map—mountainous. I found a narrow strip of green from Pearisburg to Blacksburg, Virginia. It looked like it might be the easiest route with less mountains.

Believe it or not, I agonized over such decisions with all these considerations and unknown possibilities swimming in my head. It's part of my contemplative personality. I can argue with myself with the best of them, but I made a decision. It was good!

Virginia Tech "Memorial Visit"

The day after my birthday was just another day of walking. Glenda said we probably would arrive in Blacksburg. She called some churches and one church, a Baptist Church, agreed to let us dry camp in their parking lot.

Little did we know what was coming that night to bless us, but also deeply touch us. When I walked into Blacksburg, life sped up considerably. Glenda phoned me to tell me that I was walking into a college community. That was exciting. Now, I would be walking through the community where Virginia Tech is located.

When we stopped for the night at the Baptist Church, we were right across the street from Virginia Tech. While Glenda prepared supper, I walked around part of the beautiful campus. After we ate, Glenda and I walked around more of the campus. As we walked, I knew there was something special about this place, but I couldn't place what it was.

As we met and visited with a mother of a student, the mother encouraged us to visit the Memorial. Bingo! I knew what it was. This was the location of a devastating shooting where thirty-two students and professors died on April 16, 2007. We visited a very moving memorial for the thirty-two people who died on campus at the hands of a lone gunman.

With our hearts touched, we rested that night, saddened by the tragedy that occurred there. But we were thankful for the courage of the Virginia Tech community to resolve that the memory of the fallen would be a basis for courage and strength for Virginia Tech in the future. The fallen would not be forgotten!

When the Rain Gets Inside...Uh Oh!

We stayed at an RV camp in Dixie Caverns, Virginia, on Saturday, August 18. We remember the stop because it rained all night. Not a hard rain, just continuous. In the morning, we had water on the floor next to our bed. Our slideout had leaked for the first time on the *Walk*. It was enough water to be concerned. We took our towels to clean up the water, pulled the slideout in, and pondered our problem.

Knowing we'd face more rain, we had to do something. Envisioning a money drain, a delay in the *Walk*, our frustrations and concerns mounted. This obstacle seemed bigger than most. (Don't they all?)

Glenda's Glimpses: Miserable Night

It was a miserable night. We were okay in the motorhome, but as soon as we walked outside, it was just wet! (Whenever we could, we would use the facilities provided, whether RV park, Walmart, church or wherever, to minimize use of our holding tanks.) So, through the wet grass in the rain we trudged. It was not only rainy, but pretty dreary being enclosed by mountainous terrain and dripping trees.

We discovered in the morning that our RV leaked. That just made the new day miserable, as well.

Encouragement from New Friends

Even with Sunday off to a bad start, I took time to visit with our RV neighbors. I'm glad I did. They were going home to a place in Kentucky where we had walked by while they were in Maine. A retired teacher, principal, and educator of all types in a very small town, he also knew RV's. He encouraged us that the leak could be fixed. We started praying to find an RV place nearby that we could get into without a long wait and large expense. We would deal with that on Monday, August 19.

With new hope, we went to church to find some needed strength. We found it. The rest of the story is in week twenty-one.

REFLECTIONS ON WEEK 20

We had a definite message to convey.

We will probably never know how far-reaching the message carried.

Our part was to faithfully proclaim it.

****

And this is love: that we walk in obedience to his commands. (2 John 1:6)

Week 21
August 19-25 – Salem, VA to Maple Grove, VA
108 Miles

Walking through History

The Rest of the Story

The "RV leak" obstacle occurred on Saturday, August 17, and concerned us all day on Sunday, August 18. RV centers in Roanoke, Virginia, were closed on Sunday. Monday, August 19, was the day for the "rest of the story."

What a day! What a story! As most stories, it had a downside, but also an upside.

The downside entered in my **journal** for August 19 included:

1) *Because of the leak, we did not put the slideout out, so we didn't have a bed. With the upper bunk full of materials for the Walk, Glenda and I slept on the "table bed." It's not made for two adults, but it worked. We're not big people, praise God.*

2) *Camping World needed a two-week notice, plus it was estimated to cost us $1,000 to repair the leak. (Two fears we had were coming to reality. Our obstacle was a **huge one!**)*

3) *Even with the RV to repair, I still needed to walk, so I walked through Salem and Roanoke that afternoon.*

The upside entered in my **journal** included:

1) *Rain stopped in the morning and stayed stopped all day.*

2) *Camping World got us in and added an awning over the slideout. Cost was $361 and work was done by 10:30 a.m. WOW!*

3) *I walked fourteen miles after lunch (12:30-6:30).*

4) *Glenda got the RV generator oil changed; the man heard our story and waived the $100 charge. Thank you! God is so good!*

5) *Met a great man at Camping World who became a friend. His wife brought us supper at the Walmart parking lot where we spent the night in Bonsock, Virginia.*

The "RV leak" obstacle was a huge one. However, the dismal possibilities we faced were defeated powerfully by the victories of the day.

The "rest of the story" was that of a glorious ending to a potentially huge obstacle.

Glenda's Glimpses: From a Big Obstacle to a Huge Blessing

What began as a huge obstacle resulted in a huge blessing. While waiting at Camping World, we met two gentlemen. One was, Charles Elkins, who shared with us about his wife's survival of cancer and gave us her CD of testimony and song.

The other gentleman's name was, Gig Edwards. We had a wonderful conversation. That night he and his wife, Susan, brought us dinner at the Walmart parking lot. It was really one of the nicest locations for a Walmart. Where we parked, we were overlooking a beautiful valley.

Chatting in Walmart "parlor"

Jim sat on the guardrail of the parking lot while we visited with Gig, Susan, and their teenage son, Dalton. That wasn't the end of our time with Gig. We were getting low on water, so two days later we met up with him and his mother-in-law to fill up with water at a little country church where they worship. Indeed, they did help us in many ways. "Thank you for being willing to be a part of God's thing."

Gig helped us out in many ways that day. Here is an **excerpt** from an email I received from Gig after asking permission to use his name in our book:

> *Glenda,*
>
> *Great to hear from you! Just got your email and I think that a book would be the best way to share such an epic adventure! We struck up a conversation about your orange shirts at Camping World and about what you were doing and what was up with your RV. At that time, we exchanged numbers just*

in case you needed anything while you were in the area; I was off for a few days and had time to help if needed (that was a God thing!) We are very proud to know you guys and to have been called of God to help and to cover you.

God Bless, and keep us in the loop!
Gig Edwards

Earlier, while we were waiting for the motorhome to get finished, we went out to see the Canadian geese in the field. Jim went running to them, and I caught the neatest picture of Jim with his arms widespread as were the wings of the geese. They looked like they were all flying off together. Couldn't have been choreographed any better.

"Flying" while waiting for repairs

> *You have to have some fun along the way.*

D-Day Memorial – Bedford, VA

On Wednesday, August 21, passing through Bedford, Virginia, we decided to visit the D-Day Memorial. People said that visiting it was a must. We visited and tears came to our eyes.

It is not located in Bedford because it's a densely populated place (5,924 in 2012 census), but because Bedford paid a price on D-Day. The town's website describes why the Memorial is located there. It's an honorable tribute to the price the town paid one day in 1944, on the beaches of Normandy.

The National D-Day Memorial in Bedford is located in the town suffering the highest per capita D-Day losses in the nation. There were nineteen friends, brothers, cousins who were killed that day, out of a town of 3,200. The Memorial honors the Allied forces that participated in the invasion of Normandy on June 6, 1944. "With its stylized English Garden, haunting invasion tableau, and striking Victory Plaza, the Memorial stands as a powerful permanent tribute to the valor, fidelity, and sacrifice of D-Day participants."[3]

I was so glad we stopped. We will always remember our visit and thank Bedford, for helping to end WWII. If you are ever in or near Bedford, Virginia, visit the Memorial, but bring your handkerchief. You'll need it.

> *Our visit was awesome. It's something every American should see. You will be touched in just a couple of hours or spend the day. It was worth it!*

---

[3] www.dday.org

Too bad every elementary school child can't go there, just to be in touch with the greatest generation. We're losing that connection with the spirit of those valiant soldiers, many in their teens, who fought, many dying, for our country. Many who lived became a foundation for our country, but that's fading. It would be nice to get their spirit back. We left there with hearts deeply touched.

Lynchburg – Victory FM Interview (Excerpt from the road)

We left about 11:00 a.m. to go to Lynchburg to pick up where I had stopped walking. At noon, we ate lunch and napped, and I started walking again about 1:20. I walked about two miles in an hour. Slow walking in town. Also, in town it can be a tricky area because it can be hard trying to find which road.

Finally, I was walking briskly, making good time and a car pulled up beside me and the man inside asked me, "Are you the person in the Billy Graham video about the Walk across America?"

I answered, "Yes I am. I'm Jim Buckley," and gave him my card.

He said, "My name is Mark Lamb, and I'm with Liberty University Broadcasting, called Victory FM radio station. I'd like to interview you. Do you have time to do that?"

Well, of course I told him that I had time to do that. He directed me to the station and I met him there after walking about a mile. It was right next to the Thomas Road Baptist Church, the late Jerry Falwell's church. He passed away in 2007. It's a huge church. Glenda and I visited it after the interview.

I called Glenda and she met me at the station and brought some of our brochures that Mark Lamb had requested. She and I were interviewed by Mark Lamb for probably forty-five minutes, but it went by rapidly. He was good as he let us talk. It was just really, really good for us. He seemed to be pleased. What a pleasant surprise being interviewed for Victory FM.

Glenda's Glimpses: "River of Delights"

I enjoyed the interview. Mark was an excellent interviewer. We have also enjoyed having contact with him some since. He also interviewed our son, Jared, over the phone, and they had a good conversation about the purpose of the *Walk*.

Jim and I were apart through much of Lynchburg but kept phone contact. When Jim was walking through a town, I didn't feel as much a need to keep in visual contact with him. I felt more secure knowing that he was walking on sidewalks and traffic wasn't so dangerous for him. I do remember a few times when I was looking for him and whizzed right by him because he had decided to go into a store without telling me. It added variety, but sometimes frustration.

Actually, walking through towns caused a problem for him because he could not make good time. Stoplights slowed him down, going into those stores slowed him down, and people slowed him down. But then that was what the *Walk* was all about–people. The "relational" Jim enjoyed it, the "conquering" Jim got frustrated. Oh, how we all battle ourselves.

I had been wanting to get a new study and was looking for a Beth Moore study to do. I was finishing up what I had been working on, so I thought if I could just find a Christian book store, maybe I could find a study. About noon, I stopped at a Walmart, just across the street from the back side of Liberty University. After lunch, Jim was headed out again.

I had to do some walking to reach my 10,000 steps for the day. I decided to walk on the other side of the street, and lo and behold, there was a Lifeway store where Beth Moore's books were sold. I had even looked on the internet to try to find a Lifeway store but did not find one–instead, I stumbled onto it. Doesn't that just beat all? Who knew? I know Who knew. Timing again.

Makes me giggle. It was one of the many little drinks from the Lord's "river of delights" (Psalm 36:8).

I had been memorizing Psalm 36:5-8. There was so much meaning in that passage for me. I don't remember why I chose the passage, but different sections meant so much to me at different times. The "river of delights" became my theme song. I would write to people maybe once a week and give them a report and prayer requests. Not long into the *Walk* I started sharing with these people (some who had been with us from the beginning and others who were added along the way) my drinks from the "river of delights," little surprises that God had for me. Things that made my heart leap–sometimes little leaps and other times, huge jumps.

On to Appomattox (Excerpt)

We had a great visit at the Appomattox Court House. We saw some slide footage about the signing of the treaty of the surrender by Lee, and just a lot of history there.

We saw the fields where Grant's forces gathered as Lee was preparing to surrender to Grant on April 9, 1865. From the history reported at the Appomattox Court House on our visit, Lee had no choice. The Civil War in Virginia was drawing to a close and his troops were struggling. The Larger War didn't end on that day at Appomattox, but that was a decisive day for the Union Army, as well as America. It was the beginning of putting the nation back together. Five days later, April 14, President Lincoln was shot by John Wilkes Booth and died the next morning.

President Lincoln is a relative in our family on the Buckley side as I am a distant cousin (seventh cousin) of President Lincoln.

Glenda's Glimpses: Empathy for Both Generals

I'm not a historian by any means, but the slide presentation was very sobering and touching. It told of a powerful General Lee who had to admit that they were done, that they could not go on. After the terms were agreed upon by both generals, General Lee was a saddened leader who marched through some of his soldiers in formation. They had high regard for him, feeling his grief and sense of defeat. That was to be expected. But what took me back was the described attitude and demeanor of General Grant. It was not one of a conquering leader. He was a man who had high regard for General Lee and empathy, sadness for this man. The presentation described a very solemn laying-down-of-arms as the Confederate soldiers rode/walked through the Union soldiers in formation. The Union soldiers displayed high respect. General Grant then scribbled a note to President Lincoln to inform him of the surrender. It was short and to the point–no glory, just information. I had empathy for both generals.

After we watched the presentation, we decided to walk around the grounds and the preserved buildings. There was a young man who was in character and uniform as a soldier from 1865. He never fell out of character and was very interesting. He also was very amusing at times. We asked if we could take his picture. He seemed to be intrigued by our using a small box to capture his image–my cell phone.

Walking through the University of Virginia (Excerpt)

I am at the beginning of the University of Virginia and will walk through it. I don't know how long this will take, but I will walk through it. It's a gorgeous day, beautiful campus, and a good day to walk.

I'm walking through forested areas, reminding me of the University of Oregon campus in Eugene, Oregon, but this campus is more wooded. The U of O campus was where Glenda and I walked on our first "unofficial" date. Memories!

Glenda's Glimpses: Too Tall

Going through Charlottesville was a challenge for me. While Jim was walking through the campus, I had to take some detours. Some actually said "detour." Other detours were because I'm so tall–the motorhome, not me. When I would see a sign that said 10', I had to find another way. You see, the motorhome is 11'6". In Kentucky, I had found a wonderful shortcut for Jim that wasn't good for me. There was no warning. I was driving on this picturesque country road when up ahead was an overpass made up of railroad ties over the road. It said 10'. I had to back up on the road, up someone's driveway, and turn around. Jim was able to keep going, but I had to find another road. Again, that's why I drove 9,000 miles and Jim walked 3,131.

Back to Charlottesville. I eventually got through town, taking this and that detour, up and down hills, and around twists and turns. It made my heart pitter patter.

REFLECTIONS ON WEEK 21

What began as a huge obstacle became a huge blessing.

There were many little surprises that God had for me, drinks from the Lord's "river of delights."

Things that made my heart leap – sometimes little leaps and other times, huge jumps.

****

They feast on the abundance of your house; You give them a drink from your river of delights. (Psalm 36:8)

Week 22

Near the East Coast

Meeting New Friends (Excerpt)

It is amazing how fast we can develop new friendships,
if we take the time.

Walter is now a good friend. I met him yesterday when he was stopping for the day, fully dressed in motorcycle gear as he and his wife are on a trip. I saw him again this morning at McDonalds in his street clothes. We had the best visit in just fifteen minutes. Talking about family, friends, and faith, we bonded.

Later while I was walking, I saw him and his wife going by on their motorcycle. I had this feeling of seeing good friends, though we just met. I thought, wow, it has not been even twenty-four hours and we're good friends, bonded through the Lord and our shared lives. He was so excited about what Glenda and I are doing.

I just made another friend. I was with the lady for no more than five minutes. Marsha Rose, an African-American woman, prayed for me and the Walk. In just five minutes, I felt so bonded. Unbelievable. She's so connected with this idea of Jesus living in your home.

I met some teenagers yesterday; one of them set up a Facebook thanking me for doing what I'm doing. This is amazing. I'm simply blown away.

There are a lot of people that the Lord is touching through this Walk. It's face to face and happens anywhere, if my heart is ready. On this Walk, I make time for people.

The message I'm getting today is, "Slow down, Jim, take time to touch more lives."

Glenda's Glimpses: Vital Connection

As we write, we pull many things out of our memories, but we are helped by journal, Facebook, camera shots, Jim's tape recorder for his excerpts, but today I realized I have another source. While I didn't keep an official journal, there was something I did. We had people that were praying for us. I would write them, sharing with them my "drinks" from the Lord's "river of delights." I would also ask them for prayer for specific concerns and needs. By the end of the *Walk*, we had about 400 prayer partners to whom I would write. I can be a "pack rat" of sorts. Well, I did not delete my prayer emails to our prayer partners. Here is one of those emails:

Hello Prayer Warriors,

I hope you realize how important your prayers are to us. I feel like I hit "the wall" this last week. I realize spiritual attack is to be expected. We heard and really connected with a sermon last Sunday. One of the illustrations was that of the giant redwoods. The trees do not have deep roots and yet they tower so high. What they do have is connection. The trees' roots intertwine with one another and literally hold one another up. Connected. I have talked about that—connecting. Your connection with the Lord on our behalf calls for our Lord Jesus' power and strength to keep us going. Some of you saw the picture on Facebook, "No stopping." It came the day after a really rough day—turmoil over continued questions about if there will be turnouts so that I can stay close to Jim, would there be wide enough shoulders for him to walk safely, what is around that next corner – a common concern through these hills as I watch Jim walk and walk and walk. Connection with you means so much. Your Facebook comments encourage and your responses to prayer updates remind us that you are out there, praying. So we can make it. Jesus is around that next corner and He is victorious!

Excerpt from the Road

We just made our first appointment for Washington, D.C., with Focus on the Family. It's going to be at 2:00 on Wednesday, September 4. This is an important visit because Focus' heart is in the home. This is the legislative branch of Focus.

The discouraging part of this afternoon is that I have been walking since a nap break at a little after 2:00. It's almost 4:00, that's two hours, and I haven't even gone four miles, yet. It has been horrendous. What I've walked has been dangerous to say the least. I'm walking fine right now, big shoulder.

We made a great contact today with George Morris, the U of Virginia football team chaplain, through Sean Willis, from Newbury Park. (George is with Fellowship of Christian Athletes.) We have more propane now. Glenda got that. So good things have happened, and we're looking forward to seeing the Shiflets.

Glenda's Glimpses: Branches and Bumpers

While Jim had his issues with the shoulders of the road, I had my own. First, I had to find a place to get some propane in Ruckersville. That went smoothly, but what didn't go smoothly was trying to find a good parking lot to sit in. It wasn't one of my best decisions by any means. I drove in thinking I would drive around the building and come out at a better place. As I went to the side of the building, it was narrow—trees with low branches on one side and parked cars on the other. I drove carefully, slowly, proud of my acquired motorhome-driving skills. That was a premature thought. The parking went around the back. What I didn't see until I got to the back was there was no outlet. I surveyed the situation and realized there was no room to turn around back there, either. I had to back up through the narrow passageway, between the trees and parked cars. I used my mirrors, backing very cautiously. I got out several times to check on branches and bumpers. I didn't want to tangle with either one. In time, I was back in the front parking area where I had to turn around after all. If anyone saw me, they didn't make themselves known, neither to help nor laugh.

Driving to Stay with Friends

At the close of the day, Glenda and I drove to see Don and Donna Shiflet, parents of Kim Rousseau, a very good friend from Newbury Park. We know the Shiflets from their visits to see their family in Newbury Park. They have been so supportive of the *Walk*, and encouraged us to "stop by" if we ended up near them. When we realized we would be close, we contacted them and they insisted that we drive to them and spend the night. We eagerly accepted their offer.

In my **journal** I wrote, *We made it to Ruckersville and drove thirty miles to Don and Donna Shiflet's home in the Shenandoah Valley. We ate delicious food, bathed (felt so good), and slept in a nice bed. Awesome! We had a wonderful night with Don and Donna, who has partial paralysis from excess radiation for cancer after the birth of their third child. She has been in a wheelchair for ten years, but her spirit is wonderful. What a delight to be with them.*

Glenda woke up in the morning at 5:00 and said, "Can we sleep in?"

I said, "It's coming, but not yet."

That would have been an ideal place just to sleep in until 8:00 or 9:00 and just stretch and have a good time, but we have a destination.

(Author's note: Glenda wanted me to assure the reader that we did shower regularly in our RV. However, when given the opportunity of a bath, we loved it.)

Glenda's Glimpses: New York Coming

It was wonderful staying with Don and Donna. We could forget the challenges for an evening. They were amazing hosts, and Donna didn't let the wheelchair slow her down. Don was so supportive of her and helpful.

They fed us some fresh produce out of their garden. I was able to get some laundry done while visiting, too.

Back on the road, I was beginning to get frustrated and a little panicked. We were starting to see a little bit of light at the end of the tunnel–New York. The kids and grandkids are all going to get to join us, but that brought pressure. Where were we going to stay? New York is very expensive. I knew we needed to have a place that would be accessible to where we would cross into New York City as a family. I knew that none of us had money spilling out of our pockets, yet we needed to all be together. There were thirteen grandkids. We needed a place that would allow us to feed all those mouths.

Then I felt the pressure of pleasing all of these beautiful offspring. That's been a problem of mine for many years. I know I can't please them all, but I sure try. I wanted it to be a good, memorable trip for all. So, out came the tour books; I searched them, the internet, maps, and any brochures I could lay my hands on. I would agonize one minute, then the next minute I would tell God that I knew He would provide.

> *My brain was swimming. It's a wonder I didn't lie awake at night, but I was too tired for that, and God was on it!*

A Walkable Rainstorm and Culpepper, Virginia (Excerpt)

It's 1:17 p.m. on August 28, day 150 of the Walk. I had said this was going to be a challenging last leg. We had the hardest rain that I've walked in yet this morning. I walked in rain from 7:15 until 11:00 a.m. I was soaked from head to toe. Sneakers were soaked. Two foot inserts were wet. I'm on my third set of shoes right now. I was soaked because the area I walked in during the downpour was where there was no shoulder, so I was walking in a river of water. Glenda tried to pick me up, but there was no way she could safely stop, so I just had to tough it out and walk on.

In the midst of the heavy rain, Marcus Marcusson called from Newbury Park to tell me about his daughter, Amelia, inviting a friend to go to a Harvest Crusade in Anaheim, and her friend accepting the Lord. The Marcussons were excited because the friend is normally a shy person, yet she publicly stepped forward to give her life to Jesus.

Getting exciting news in the midst of the heaviest downpour? I think God might have been reminding me that He is changing lives even when I get pre-occupied with my own issues.

Right after the downpour and exciting phone call, the rain and the traffic let up. I stopped because I saw a dead animal. I hadn't seen this kind of animal on the Walk. It was a beaver. I pulled it off the road. It was pretty heavy. I then had a moment of silence for this big beaver, sad he'd been killed.

Culpepper, Virginia, was unknown to me, but not anymore. I'm not a Civil War historian, but we drove in last night to spend the night at Walmart in Culpepper, a Civil War town. We received a dinner invitation from Dr. Joseph Peck, and accepted.

Joseph, a fifty-six year old anesthesiologist (currently not in a practice), has a congenital hip issue. His life goal is to reach five billion people for Jesus, and he has been at it just for a few years. He invited a friend, Virginia, to meet us as we ate dinner. She is a writer and wrote a historical novel about Culpepper in the Civil War.

Culpepper is a town of 15,000 people, but in the war it was the most heavily traveled road and city in the war, as the North and the South were trying to gain the upper hand in Culpepper. It was a critical passageway. Virginia had all kinds of stories. Joseph treated us to dinner at a Thai Restaurant and then had to leave to go to a meeting.

We talked with Virginia about the Walk as she was fascinated with that. We switched gears to all sorts of things, and then ended up with Virginia giving us an informative and historic tour of Culpepper.

Glenda's Glimpses: Seeing the Sights

What an evening it was. Virginia was very vivacious and had stories to tell. In fact, she took us in her car around Culpepper to see the sights. She was so excited about the history that she had included in her historical novel, *Marching Through Culpepper*. She just glowed. Dr. Peck was the type of person who draws that out of people–to dream and then make it happen. Culpepper was quite momentous, for sure.

The Ballas Family

On August 29, I started walking toward Manassas, Virginia, and walked through the battlefield of Manassas, one of the first ground battles of the Civil War. We met up with Dr. Barry Bryson, the pulpit minister of the Manassas Church of Christ. He met with Glenda first. They were looking over directions to Washington, D.C., and he was giving her suggestions. Then I arrived and we talked.

One of his homeschooling families of the church came to meet us. It was a mother named Julie, and three of her children, Cameron, Lacey, and Bryan, twelve, nine, and six years old. They met with us for over an hour at the Stone House, a very special part of the Manassas battlefield. The House served as a first aid station, but also later as a place for soldiers to eat. We were there a long time.

Glenda's Glimpses: She Finished Our Laundry

We had the joy of meeting the rest of the Ballas family that weekend. It really did this "mom/grandma's" heart good. After church, we went out to their house. We met Steve and their year and a half old twin boys, Brady and Blake. You see, we also have five kids with two of them being twins. We went back into church with Julie and two of the kids that evening, knowing I still had laundry to do. When we got back to their house, their oldest daughter had finished our laundry and helped Steve fix dinner for us. They were such a blessing from the "river of delights."

With the Ballas family

REFLECTIONS ON WEEK 22

There are a lot of people that the Lord is touching through this Walk.

On this Walk, I make time for people.

The message I'm getting today is:
"Slow down, Jim, take time to touch more lives."

Jesus is around that next corner and He is victorious!

****

The mind of man plans his way, but the LORD directs his steps.
(Proverbs 16:9 NASB)

Week 23

September 2-8 – Fair Lakes, VA to Joppa, MD
71 miles

Nation's Capital

Closer to the Finish Line

As we began Week 23 of the *Walk*, we were exhausted, but equally energized by how close we were to our destination, New York City. As we prepared to walk through our nation's capital, excitement was carrying us through the exhaustion. We'd come so far and were so close to the finish line, so we pressed on with Jesus, and we would cross the finish line with Him in a few weeks. We were also excited that we were one week closer to our **Most Memorable Moment** that was coming in New York City.

Glenda's Glimpses: Across America Already

We were really looking forward to this week. Jared flew in on Sunday evening and our friend and lead pastor, Ken LaMont, flew in Tuesday. Then the BGEA video team was to meet up with us on Wednesday.

There was another reason this was special for me. Jim actually had already walked across America, coast to coast. While we weren't finished, it just felt good. It seemed like Washington would have been a great place to finish, but Jesus had more for us. We wouldn't have missed the "more" for anything in the world.

RV Goes to Washington

In my **journal** on Monday, September 2, I wrote: *We left at 8:30 a.m. with Jared driving us in his rental car to D.C. and to Arlington National Cemetery to visit the burial site of Stephanie's uncle (her dad's brother). The visit meant a lot for Steph's dad for us to do that. (Stephanie is Jared's wife.) Then we drove a possible path which we might drive the RV through D.C., but it was nothing that excited me. After that trial drive, I was more concerned than ever about maneuvering our 22-foot RV through some very narrow D.C. streets, always needing to be aware of the eleven and a half foot height of the RV.*

Due to traffic, narrow streets, and new territory, we decided it was best to have Glenda on her iPad to help direct us, while I drove. With the Lord guiding us, I slowly and cautiously drove our RV through D.C. streets to 16th & Decatur Church of Christ parking lot that would be our home for the four nights in D.C. I was thrilled just to get the RV in so quickly and easily. My **journal** entry stated, *I drove the RV to Constitution and 14th to Decatur like a charm.*

We met Ed Wilson, minister of the church, who would be our host while in Washington, D.C. He provided us with a safe, close spot to park our RV at no cost.

The closest RV place was $65 a night and was about twenty minutes or more out of town. From the church by bus we could be in town in a few minutes. It was a great place. We met Ed's wife, Carolyn, marvelous people. She can sing, and did (at our request) as we stood in the church parking lot– what a beautiful voice. They helped to make it a wonderful week.

Tuesday in D.C.

On Tuesday, September 3, all our D.C. people were arriving. We left the church parking lot, drove to the hotel where Pastor Ken LaMont was staying. Picking him up, we then went to get our Metrorail passes for traveling to where we had left off on the *Walk*. By 1:30 p.m., we had walked through the outskirts of D.C. and ended up at Arlington Cemetery. We took a break before we walked across the Arlington Memorial Bridge into D.C. Ken, Jared, Glenda, and I had already walked eight miles. We ate and rested before walking around D.C., seeing more of the sights.

The BGEA Team arrived late in the afternoon on Tuesday. Kevin, Tracy, and Jeremy had trouble finding parking, but met us near the White House. They began filming right away and took a lot of footage at the fence, viewing the White House. We saw the beautiful garden and lawn area. Security was tight, but we expected that. There were a lot of people, but we were able to get some good videos.

We walked to the Lincoln Memorial and filmed on the steps. When we went inside the Memorial, a security guard escorted the BGEA Team out as there was no videoing allowed in the Memorial. The guard was nice, but firm. Photos, yes, but no videoing. We had some great footage of the Lincoln Memorial and visited with two families about "why" the filming, and "why" the *Walk*. One family had a son who was a Christian. His parents were excited about his being a Christian, though they didn't claim to be Christians. The son had just been baptized and the parents were thrilled. We were, too.

That evening, the team took us to a special eating place in D.C. that was famous for a special "hot chili." It was a delicious meal and provided us with a relaxing time to get more acquainted. It was a good first day of filming the walk across D.C. as a key part of the *Walk* across America.

Focus on the Family in D.C.

The *Walk* was pre-empted by communication we had with Focus on the Family. We had a half-hour visit scheduled to meet with Timothy Goeglein, Vice President of External Relations in Washington, D.C. We discovered him to be a warm and brilliant man. Only three of us were scheduled to meet with him due to a small office, but he said Ken LaMont could join Glenda, Jared, and me. He also graciously allowed the BGEA Team to video some of the visit which he extended to about thirty-five minutes. He was a fascinating man who was so supportive of the *Walk*.

My Cousin Has Connections

My cousin, Carleen Morris, impacted our visit to Washington, D.C. by opening some doors to people in "high places." Of the three special visits we had in D.C., she opened the door to two, stemming from many years on Capitol Hill working for Representative Richard Gephardt from Missouri, then for Senator Joe Lieberman, from Connecticut.

Glenda, though exhausted, decided to join me with two appointments I had made through my cousin. The first meeting was with Clarine Nardi Riddle, a former attorney general in Connecticut, who was the Senator's Chief of Staff in the Senate and now works with Senator Joe Lieberman in the Kasowitz law firm; the Senator retired from Congress at age seventy-one. He works at the law firm as an independent and internal investigator for clients, and the law firm has also encouraged him to continue speaking out on the issues of the day in his unique voice on public policy issues. Ms. Riddle also told us about a new group, called No Labels, that she helped co-found that is trying to end the gridlock in Congress and start solving the country's problems by helping congressional leaders understand they can work together and solve problems even when they don't agree on each issue. We had a fascinating visit with Ms. Riddle, who was an extremely gifted and clear communicator.

From Senator Lieberman's office, we took a bus to Capitol Hill several blocks away. We had to go through tight screening and security to get to the Senate offices. Once inside the Senate building, we walked to the Senate Chaplain's office where we met the Chaplain's Chief of Staff, Mrs. Lisa Schultz. She shared with us that she was a disciple of Jesus. Chaplain Barry Black was not in that day. She showed us his office and pictures of him and his family, and shared the joy she had with working with a man so committed to his faith and his country. We were there about twenty minutes, had a good visit, and were able to get a glimpse of the life of the Chaplain of the Senate. I shared with Mrs. Schulz that my cousin had hoped that I might lead the opening prayer in the Senate while I was in D.C. However, that wasn't possible this time because the Senate was not in session. She smiled and suggested that it could be possible sometime later. When she asked if I would be interested, I answered, "Absolutely."

Glenda's Glimpses: Every Home

It was amazing to me to be able to park our motorhome in the middle of Washington, then to have Jared staying with us. He had been so involved with the *Walk*. He was manning the Inviting America Home Facebook page, posting almost every day.

An important prayer

One of my favorite pictures is when I took a close-up of Jim looking through the fence at the White House, Jared posted across the picture, "Praying for EVERY HOME in America." Jared did a fantastic job keeping us visible and really augmenting our message.

Ebenezers Coffeehouse

On Wednesday morning, September 4, we met with the BGEA Team and began a full day of filming. We were all over D.C., even walking two times across the Arlington National Memorial Bridge. Filming was much harder than I thought. The crew needed the right light and angles. They filmed me walking into the city, and filmed around different places, spending a lot of time filming and interviewing Ken, Jared, Glenda, and me at the Martin Luther King Memorial.

While spending so much time at the Memorial, we had some great moments meeting people like the VanDoren family from Texas and Tennessee. They ended up praying for us. Dr. VanDoren is a pediatric surgeon who goes to Haiti and does pediatric heart surgery. He even suggested that our daughter-in-law, Stephanie (a nurse), look into working with him as a nurse in Haiti–awesome.

I talked with Gertie, a ninety-year-old woman, who was sitting on a park bench. She was just fascinated that we were walking across America. After the BGEA Team left, Ken, Jared, Glenda, and I went to the Ebenezers Coffeehouse. We met Jodi, a social media person for the National City Community Church that owns the coffeehouse. Mark Batterson, well-known author and speaker, is the pastor. Nicole, a woman we met at Ebenezers, and many others were fascinated with the *Walk*, so we talked and visited, taking pictures of us with them before we left. Then we went to eat at Ted's Bulletin and Ken treated, relaxing and reminiscing about the day of filming in the nation's capital. We got to the RV late, but blessed at the end of a very long, but fruitful day for the Lord.

Glenda's Glimpses: Defining Moment

While in Culpepper, Virginia, Dr. Joseph Peck had urged us to go to Ebenezer's Coffeehouse. That was a divine appointment that led us to a defining moment for me–finding the book, *The Circle Maker,* by Mark Batterson. I picked up the book on display and was so intrigued by it. We bought it. While Jim, Jared, and Ken talked, I was in the corner reading. After leaving D.C., I read through the book on my many turnouts. I was so impacted, it changed my prayer life. I have experienced some amazing answers to prayer due to the change.

> *God had been going before us time and time again. We certainly never walked alone!*

Deer in D.C.?

Who would expect to see deer in "downtown" Washington, D.C.? Not I. However, on the morning after our second night dry camping in the Church of Christ parking lot, Jared claimed that he saw deer in the early morning. Right! I was certain he was exhausted from his trip from Utah and then a busy day across D.C. He insisted he wasn't dreaming.

On the third night, my wife also saw the deer. Now, I had two people losing their minds.

On the fourth night, I lost my mind, as I saw the deer. Really! I saw two fawns and a doe. Mom and her two kids. In D.C.? *Yes.*

Before we left D.C., Ed Wilson laughed and assured us we were not seeing things. Deer frequent his church parking lot. The doe (mom) and her two fawns are quite interesting he told us. Since the Wilson's live in the church, they said that they saw the deer quite often. One morning in particular, the mom was with her two fawns. She looked at them for a moment, then left. They followed, but when she turned and gave a "long look," they froze. Turning around, they walked back to the parking lot and stayed a long time, until she returned.

Not only did we see deer, but we also saw a doe who could write a training book on how to raise obedient children.

Glenda's Glimpses: New Challenges

It wasn't easy for Jared to stay with us in the motorhome. He had stayed with us in Arizona, so he knew what he was getting into. We made up the bed where the table was and it wasn't long enough for him. He would do what he could to try to get comfortable. Then to add to it, it was very warm. We didn't turn on the air conditioning overnight, probably because we would have turned on the noisy generator. I was always afraid we would disturb neighbors. So, it stands to reason that Jim would doubt that Jared saw deer. We found out later that the park just a few blocks away was overrun with deer. Who would have thought in the middle of D.C.?

Driving out of Washington wasn't too bad. It was an old residential area. I did a lot of turning down side streets, driving around the block. Once we hit the city limits leaving Washington, it became a challenge. It was very congested and a bit tangled so that side streets and around the block didn't work very well. It certainly was different than driving across the Mojave Desert or the wilderness of New Mexico. Just when I would get the hang of one area of the country, a new area brought new challenges.

Baltimore–John Hopkins Hospital

On Saturday, September 7, I walked on Hwy 40 through Baltimore. It was an ethnically mixed area (Hispanic and African-American) that looked like one of the poorer parts of any major city. We had been advised that this highway would be a safer part to walk through than farther south which was described as more dangerous. The people I met were pleasant and friendly, but the surroundings included remnants of broken bottles and trash, plus many dilapidated apartments. Walking that day was one of the tougher parts of our *Walk*. It was not a reflection of Baltimore, but the fact that I was walking through a rough part of a major city. All major cities that I have visited have areas like this one. The difference is that I don't normally walk through them. I did talk with a group of young people from a nearby church that was holding a fund-raiser for their church. They were outstanding youth.

I did enjoy walking under the huge sign indicating the world famous John Hopkins Hospital. What an honor for Baltimore to have such a hospital.

Glenda's Glimpses: Not Walking Here

Coming in from the West, I found a neat Baltimore sign on the nice residential street where we entered the city proper. It took a little bit to get a picture of Jim when he got there. Not far from there, we came to John Hopkins Hospital. Their big hospital sign stretches over the street on a skyway walking bridge.

Walking through famous hospital

Then, as is true in the inner city, things changed. The area just seemed to look more and more dangerous. Jim just didn't blend in with his redhead complexion. Neither did the motorhome. I would turn down side streets to turn around and park facing the street on which Jim was walking. Each street I turned down felt less safe. Finally, I'd had enough, called Jim and told him he was not walking here. He needed to use his bank miles and we needed to get out of there. Jim agreed. It's amazing that there could be such a rough area near such a beautiful hospital.

We had been in conversation with Brandi Campbell, who had grown up with our son, Jason. She lived near Washington, D.C., and took the day off from work and sat in the motorhome with me as Jim walked. It was fun to get to visit with her. We met up with her again in Joppa, Maryland, to attend church.

Mountain Christian Church, Joppa, Maryland

We arrived at Mountain Christian Church on Saturday, September 8, late in the afternoon. We parked, then attended a special mission night the church was having celebrating all the mission teams from the church that had served in all parts of the world over the summer. Mountain is a dynamic church, with Pastor Ben Cacharias leading a ministry that is impacting thousands for Jesus in the Joppa area.

We met John Sarno, former worship pastor of Mountain, who was serving as the church's worship consultant, helping other churches improve their worship ministry. In addition, he is an adjunct professor, like I am, with TCM International Institute in Austria. John invited us to Sunday lunch and his wife, Pam, met us at the church and drove us to their home. They invited Brandi to come, too.

In 2004, while our church in Newbury Park was helping fund the expansion of a facility for the TCM library in Austria, Pam was the person who was putting the inner working of the library together for that expansion. We had worked together, though we had never met until the *Walk*. We had John, Pam, and Brandi sign our *Walk* quilt before we left.

What a small world. What an awesome God we serve.

REFLECTIONS ON WEEK 22

Praying for EVERY HOME in America.

Jim was called to walk across America to touch hearts and homes for Jesus.

****

"He who receives you receives me, and he who receives me receives the one who sent me." – Jesus (Matthew 10:40)

Week 24
September 9-15 – Joppa, MD to Along Hwy 130, NJ
97.1 Miles

Big Cities and Small Places

Glenda's Glimpses: Off Chesapeake Bay

On Monday, we headed north from Joppa. We landed that evening at Bar Harbor RV Park on the Bush River off the Chesapeake Bay. We were able to fill propane, fill water, dump, and do laundry. Our motorhome was just a few feet from the water–beautiful.

Jim's quiet time on the Bay

I took a picture of Jim sitting on a bench by the water reading his Bible. It was another "drink from His river of delights."

A Call from Home

My family called from California on Tuesday, September 10, to inform us that my brother, Larry, had passed away that afternoon after years of failing health. Being advised earlier in the week of his situation, Glenda and I had decided that we would fly home to be with our family for Larry's funeral. Larry was seventy-four years old. He passed away after some severe complications culminating years of physical problems. Our hearts were sad, but we were thankful that he was at rest from his struggles.

Three Homes

On September 11, we came to the Delaware Memorial Bridge, a beautiful bridge. I couldn't walk it as there was no walkway at all, so I drove across the bridge, then continued walking on the other side. Glenda was glad I drove. It was a very big bridge. We saw flags flying at half-mast on September 11, as America promised to "never forget." America did not and will not forget.

We had lunch that day in Wilmington, Delaware, with Josh and Christine Robinson, friends of our son, Daniel, and his wife Charity, while living in Idaho. It was great meeting them and taking time to visit with a wonderful young family. Then we drove back and I continued walking where I had stopped. We camped at the Bethel Baptist Church in Penns Grove, New Jersey, for the night.

In the morning, we met Mike, who was a builder, completing a home he had built. Later, I met Marlene, who said she was an evangelist. She told me she wanted to walk across America and pumped me for ideas. Of the three homes represented by these three contacts, Mike's was broken by a failed marriage;

Marlene's home had also been hit by a dissolved marriage; Josh and Christine had a wonderful home and marriage. Jesus lives in their home. My heart broke for Mike and Marlene, and I just prayed as I walked, that more homes in America would have Jesus living in them like Josh and Christine's.

Jesus is the difference maker and brings hope to every home where He lives. That's our message. We saw evidence of that message. We are walking to share that message.

Glenda's Glimpses: MMM Coming

Josh and Christine were now living in Pennsylvania. Daniel and Josh had taught and coached basketball together in a small town in Idaho. They were pretty proud that they had coached Shea McClellin when he was in high school. He was drafted by the Chicago Bears in 2012.

Delightful family

Their toddler entertained us; his siblings were in school, so he had the floor. As a grandma, I always gravitate to such families. We can see why Daniel and Charity were such good friends with them. It was a little bit like being with our kids. It wouldn't be long and we would be! Our **MMM** was coming!

Jim spoke to the Wednesday night kids' club at the church where we parked in Penns Grove. Even though people are the focus of the *Walk*, it was hard to do things like that after Jim's full day of walking; but we did it. Although the historical sites would have been interesting in Philadelphia, we opted not to go on that side of the river because of the dangers of walking through the city. I think we were more focused on destination than history at that point. We had loved the other historical areas we had been able to visit, but we could see an end in sight–so onward!

Big Day – Kevin and Sherry in New Jersey

September 12 was a long day of walking. I only walked nineteen miles, but in 91-94 degrees plus humidity, dripping with sweat, I was exhausted–possibly from the long, long walk of months catching up with us, but also the news of my brother's death–I was drained emotionally.

Our spirits were lifted at the end of the day when we completed the *Walk* and drove to Millstone Township, New Jersey, to stay for a few days with Kevin and Sherry (Flynn) McSweeney. Sherry was a member of Newbury Park First Christian Church and a very good friend of ours. A young widow, she recently renewed an acquaintance from her past, Kevin McSweeney, and they married in June. We were excited to see them and welcomed their gracious gift of hospitality. They fed us, and we visited into the evening, having a fantastic time. It was the perfect end to a very hard day on the *Walk*.

Kevin would be instrumental in our *MMM* as he gave us advice, as we planned to walk as a family across the huge and famous George Washington Bridge from New Jersey to New York City.

Day of MMM Planning in Secaucus, New Jersey

People sometimes are concerned about whether Friday the thirteenth is good or bad. Not us. Friday, September 13, was a very good day for us!

We drove the RV to Secaucus, New Jersey, to see if the hotel we had tentatively booked for the family and friends would be okay. It was clean and newly refurbished, had large rooms, a complimentary breakfast, and kitchenettes in each room. All these were essentials for families staying from four to seven days. A Walmart was nearby, plus a Sam's Club. Several restaurants were close by as well. We met the manager and liked him, but the best news was the bus.

The New York City bus stopped across the street from the hotel and went straight into the New York Times Square terminal. We took the bus into New York, taking only ten minutes. It was $3.60 roundtrip for seniors! It's great to be "mature."

We spent the day in New York City, seeing the Duffy Stairs at Times Square, visiting the Times Square Church, meeting and talking with Edward, a security person at the church. We walked to Whole Foods near Central Park, walking through the park to catch the subway to the George Washington Bridge.

It's huge! Actually awesome! It spans the Hudson River and hundreds of cars and trucks stream across it. We walked up to the walkway which the family would take across the bridge.

Glenda stopped me and said, "I don't think this is a good idea. Some in the family might not be able to walk this bridge."

While talking, I realized she was not only one of the "some," she would be the "leader." I knew she didn't like heights and the bridge is over 200 feet above the Hudson River. I convinced her to "try it," so we carefully walked out on the narrow walkway from the New York side. After talking more, she agreed to walk further, which was good because the walkway widens after reaching the first cable section. That was better for Glenda, but not great, yet.

After "experiencing" the bridge for the first time, we took the subway back to the bus terminal at Times Square and back to the hotel in Secaucus. The return bus trip took a little longer in heavy traffic, but still very good.

We journeyed back to Millstone Township, arriving at 10:00 p.m. after a long, hard, but very productive day. We concluded that the hotel was very good for us and confirmed our booking for the rooms. We had a place to stay for several days in the New York area with knowledge of transportation, lodging, and food. We would learn more in following "undercover" trips, but our first one was a success and put our minds at ease.

Thank you, Lord, for leading the way again! MMM
was coming, one day, one step at a time!

Glenda's Glimpses: Pitter Patter Moments

My mind was put at ease with our exploratory trip. It was nice to find that the hotel was a good decision. The location was wonderful. It was a very nice area. It was such a good place for the families, especially the children. This grandma was satisfied. I had made reservations in four other hotels around, but we decided quickly to let them go. God's guidance in my research had paid off. To top it all off, it was about a third the cost of staying in New York City. The manager was so accommodating. He invited us to park the RV while we went into the city to investigate for the day.

The one rough thing about the day was driving into the area. Turnpikes tangled all over. I counted eight lanes one way on one of them, but it wasn't as crowded as LA freeways. I tell people it is like a necklace all tangled. We had some pitter patter moments coming in because my iPad wasn't matching up with the signs. Every time I saw Lincoln Tunnel on the sign, I panicked and sent us off another way which meant we had to go around. I did not want to go into the Lincoln Tunnel and end up in Manhattan in our RV! I finally realized we had to take the route that said Lincoln Tunnel, but would get off before the tunnel. They didn't teach me this on the farm—two-lane roads or better yet, country roads, some paved, some not. I'm sure glad we went from West to East. It would have been awful to start here!

Now with all that said, we found some beautiful areas in New Jersey. I was reminded by someone that it is "The Garden State." At Kevin and Sherry's house, we saw deer and wild turkey in their yard. It was a wonderful stay and they were such welcoming hosts.

Times Square Church in New York City

After a day of rest on Saturday for Glenda and me, while Kevin and Sherry took a pre-planned trip to Lancaster, Pennsylvania, we woke up early on Sunday to drive to New York City to attend the Times Square Church. Kevin drove. Kevin is amazing. He is a former Marine, now a member of the Port Authority, and currently a leader of the painting crew for the George Washington Bridge. Yes, he works with crews painting all of the bridge, a thirteen-year project.

Born in the Bronx, he knows New York. That was obvious as we drove early into New York to "get a seat" at a very prominent church. Edward, the security guard, had told us to get to the church early. We left at 7:15 a.m., arriving at 8:30 a.m.; just a few people were there. We got a good seat and watched as people poured in to fill the church for the 10:00 a.m. service.

It's a magnificent church located in one of the original theaters in New York City. We were told it's the only theater that is still original, not being remodeled, just kept looking beautiful.

At 10:00 a.m. when the stage curtain parted, our eyes were caught by a full choir loft with our ears coming alive as the music began. We rose from our seats as the spirited praise singing began. I looked at Kevin and he smiled. Raised a Roman Catholic, this was different from what he had experienced in church. The glorious morning was filled with powerful music, wonderful people, excellent preaching, and a "taste" of church in New York. Kevin and Sherry both affirmed how much they enjoyed the morning.

Kevin drove us around, showing us the George Washington Bridge from the New Jersey side, where the family would begin the *Walk* on October 4. It was a wider beginning to the bridge. Glenda liked that. We saw where the family would meet to begin the *Walk* at Hudson Terrace in Fort Lee. We hadn't decided, yet, how we would get from our hotel to Hudson Terrace.

Then back to McSweeney's home for a nap and watching football. Kevin, an avid New York Giants' fan, was disappointed as his Giants lost to the Denver Broncos. I was happy as my Chicago Bears won their game in the last second.

While Glenda and I had a "*Walk* phone meeting" with Jared (Communications Manager) and Leslie Haggard (Home Coordinator for the *Walk*), Kevin and Sherry brought us sandwiches.

Glenda: Jim and I were in two different rooms so that it was easier to talk on the phone. Jim left his room for a few minutes, leaving his unfinished sandwich. When he came back, his sandwich was gone! He didn't remember eating it. He didn't. We finally figured out that Kevin and Sherry's dog, Tubbs, had helped himself–it wasn't the last time.

There was absolutely no limit to how wonderful these friends were, and Tubbs just added some fun memories.

Sunday in New York was a wonderful day thanks to the Lord providing us with people like Kevin and Sherry.

REFLECTIONS ON WEEK 24

Jesus is the difference maker.
He brings hope to every home where He lives.
That's our message.
We are walking to share that message.

****

We have this hope as an anchor for the soul, firm and secure.
(Hebrews 6:19a)

Week 25

Home with Family and Friends

The Trip Home for My Brother's Funeral

G lenda and I flew home on Monday, September 16, then drove up
to Madera on Tuesday, September 17, to be with family at Larry's
funeral. It was good to be with family for his service. Larry Hill was born
on January 25, 1939, and died on September 10, 2013, at the age of seventy-four. He was my brother by marriage, when his mom and my dad married on August 5, 1958. When our two families merged, Larry was nineteen,
and I was twelve. He is survived by his wife, Louise, of fifty-two years, and
his son, Steven, daughter-in-law, Tonya, and their two children, Leslie and
Ryan, Larry's grandchildren.

Larry's funeral was a tribute to his life. The service featured a young lady
singing "Happy Trails," as he was western to the core. He was a huge John
Wayne fan. We were so glad we were able to be with family during this special moment honoring a brother who was a special part of our lives. We flew
back to Newark on Wednesday, September 18, to resume the *Walk*.

Glenda's Glimpses: Family Ties

I was very intimidated when I first met Jim's large family in 1966, but they were very warm and welcoming. Jim's mom was a faithful prayer warrior. She taught me some things about prayer. For one, I could call her with a concern that needed prayer. She would tell me she would pray then tell me it would be okay. Also, she taught me faithfulness in praying for each of the kids and grandkids by name every day which I now do.

The brothers made me feel right at home with their teasing. They were good at it. So was Jim's dad and Jim himself–it ran deep. Larry seemed to have a twinkle in his eye most of the time. What was interesting to me was that he liked opera. That seemed an unusual combination with his love for John Wayne.

It was so good to be able to spend time with family we hadn't seen in a long time. Family alone made it a large service, but there were so many in the community that highly respected Larry. The chapel was full.

God's impeccable timing in going to the funeral allowed for something special.

Remember how we were able to get a picture of our grandson Ryan's grave in North Carolina because of the downpour? Since we were home, I was able to go through a small box of memoirs for our stillborn son, Jeremy Stephen. In it, I found a beautiful article in the church newsletter that Jim had written thirty-six years earlier. He was pastor of the church and wrote about Jeremy. So, I made twenty-five copies to go with the twenty-five pictures of Ryan's grave. Each person in the family, babies included, had a copy to carry across the George Washington Bridge. They were both represented on that walk. Thank you, Jesus, for special moments because of Your timing.

Dog Alert! Where are my carob chips?

I am allergic to chocolate. For years, I battled that allergy and ate chocolate, especially M&M's, because I liked them. Yes, it caused my asthma to affect my breathing and activated my sinuses. Finally, I gave up the battle and being a radical, I switched to carob. After years of eating carob, I retrained my taste buds, so that now I love carob, eating primarily carob chips.

On the *Walk,* I found stores a couple of times that had carob chips and splurged, stocking up on enough to last me for several days. One of the splurges came on our flight home from my brother's funeral. I bought almost two cups of the chips and packed them away to enjoy occasional treats on the final leg of the *Walk.*

Kevin McSweeney picked us up in Newark on September 18, and we got to bed late at 11:00 p.m., doing things to allow us to get an early start to resume the *Walk.* Good plan, but good plans don't always work.

The next morning, we were up at 6:00 a.m., ready to leave by 9:00 a.m. to resume walking. Kevin and Sherry had left for work earlier. As we prepared to leave the McSweeney house, we noticed Tubbs, one of their dogs, didn't look well. We saw that he had thrown up in several places. He had eaten something that didn't agree with him, and it looked like chocolate.

We called Kevin who was alarmed as they have chocolate in the house, but they keep it hidden because it can be deadly for a smaller dog. As we watched Tubbs, I decided to have some carob chips, but couldn't find them. Glenda said she thought they were on the bed. They were, but not now.

Glenda remembered seeing a paper bag on the hall floor and wondered where that came from. She threw it away. Then she realized what had happened. Tubbs had eaten two cups of carob chips. I couldn't blame him because they are good, but now he was sick.

We waited at the house until Sherry got home from a business meeting in Richmond, Virginia, about 3:00 p.m. By that time, Tubbs was feeling better after vomiting ten times. I felt worse because I lost my chips (and so did Tubbs), but at least Tubbs and I bonded. We both like carob chips.

We were productive while waiting, doing laundry, servicing the RV, and napping. We left about 3:00 p.m., and I was able to walk over five miles before stopping for the night. It was a memorable day, all about Tubbs and chips. With Tubbs around, you never let "the chips fall where they may" or he'll eat them and yuk! You know the rest of the story.

My *Walk* is "Trumped by Trudy" (37,000 miles)

I confess. After walking over 3,000 miles, I was beginning to get a little proud, feeling like I was something special.

Be careful if pride ever begins growing in you because the Bible teaches, "Pride goes before... a fall" (A common abbreviation of Proverbs 16:18).

I had my "fall" in New Jersey when we stopped at the Black Forest Acres Natural Foods, in East Windsor, New Jersey. I phoned Glenda and told her to join me at a health food store. It was a good one. When she arrived, we met a seventy-eight-year-old clerk, Traute (Trudy) Ringwald, who announced that she also was a walker after Glenda proudly told her I had walked 3,000 miles across America. Traute took us to a spot in the store that displayed many awards and badges indicating her many walks that had covered 60,000 km which is over 37,000 miles. Wow! I was excited to meet her, realizing I had only 34,000 miles to go to catch her.

Trudy, the "real" walker

It was fun meeting her, however, plus getting some healthy snacks at the health food store. No carob chips, though.

Glenda's Glimpses: Bouquet for Me

I had a **Very Memorable Moment** along the highway. I had seen so many kinds of turnouts, but this one was indeed special. It was fall and there was orange appearing all around besides the orange on Jim's shirt. I saw parking places along some businesses and there was one that was right next to a nursery. It was so nice because there was a large enough space so I could pull right up to it.

I stopped the motorhome and looked out the window to the right and saw the most gorgeous flowers, including a sea of purple mums. I started crying. I don't mean I sniffled and teared, I mean I boohooed. I started bawling and couldn't stop. Then was when I realized I had been under a lot of strain.

God's bouquet for Glenda

I gained composure, went into the store, and thanked one of the owners (family-run business) and started crying again (just a little bit). She gave me a big hug and we chatted about what we were doing. I went back out to the motorhome and waited for Jim to walk by, enjoying the beautiful floral display. It was like God said to me, "Glenda, I know it's been hard on you, so here is a bouquet just for you." Thank you, Father, for caring so much.

REFLECTIONS ON WEEK 25

God's impeccable timing in going to the funeral allowed for something special.

God said, "Glenda, here's a bouquet just for you."

****

Be careful if pride ever begins growing in you because the Bible teaches that Pride goes before a ...fall. (Proverbs 16:18)

Week 26

September 23-29 – Hamilton, NJ to Secaucus, NJ
75 Miles

The Homestretch

Walked Past Rutgers

On Monday, September 23, Glenda was trying to find the best road with a walking shoulder, so we started on Hwy 130, transferred to Hwy 1, then on to Hwy 27. Glenda thought Hwy 27 looked better on the iPad, but we learned that speculation from an iPad can be risky. It wasn't a better road, and it actually took us through some "questionable" areas regarding safety for me as I walked.

The route took me through an area where I was seeing a big letter "R" in red everywhere. I was getting close to city campus of Rutgers University, which also has a country campus where Ashley, Sherry McSweeny's daughter, attends.

Walking close to the campus was another of the surprises that we experienced along the *Walk*. These surprises added a little spark to the routine of walking. Some days life needs a little extra spark.

Glenda's Glimpses: Best Route

I used every possible form of trying to find the best route. I had maps galore, usually at least two different kinds for each state or area, state atlases, which gave more detail about possible roads, and, of course, my iPad. The iPad was great on showing possible side roads. If I went to "hybrid" view, I could see an aerial view of the map. There was another website that I would use on the laptop–Street View. You could give it cross streets, and it would show an actual picture of the street. I could move it forward and back on the street. That did help me to see if it would be a good place to walk and drive, but that didn't always predict everything. Early on, I would sometimes drive ahead and check it out, but here it was getting so congested. The streets around Rutgers were narrow and tricky, but I made it!

God went before us and was always with us.

MMM – Get a Cab!

Getting close to our *MMM*, Glenda and I scouted out the possibility of using our RV as a shuttle, picking up our family and friends as they arrived at the Newark Airport. Our scouting expedition took us to the airport, and then we drove back to our hotel in Secaucus. We made it, but driving the RV on the bumpy and busy turnpike roads was not simple. Add the confusing (to us) turnpike signs and connections led us to a good decision.

We informed our arriving family members and friends to take a shuttle or cab to get from the airport to the hotel when they arrived, rather than our shuttling them. It was a very, very good decision.

Walking to the Bridge

Wednesday, September 25, was a Hallelujah Day! I wrote in my journal for that day (in big letters), *Hallelujah! We're at the George Washington Bridge.*

Glenda joined me walking that day starting at Hoboken, New Jersey, hometown of Frank Sinatra. We took a bus from our hotel to Hoboken to begin walking fifteen miles to Fort Lee, New Jersey, and the George Washington Bridge. This beautiful and majestic bridge would be the bridge our family would walk on October 4, to get from New Jersey to New York.

It was a beautiful day for a walk along the Hudson River overlooking the skyline of New York City. We passed many memorable sights including a 9/11 Memorial. I was so proud of Glenda that she was able to walk the fifteen miles and walk it with a backpack.

Glenda's Glimpses: The Walk Together

I was so excited for the day. I had searched the internet for walking routes and I found one! (Busy again.) It was called the Hudson River Loop Walk. It gave detailed instructions including walking across a specific parking lot. I printed it and carried it. Someone we met took a picture of us with the Hudson River and New York City skyline in the background. I just noticed a few days ago that I was holding a sheet of paper—our instructions. We followed it and it worked!

Walking along the Hudson River

It was a gorgeous day, the sky so blue and the air warm with just enough autumn nip to keep us from getting too warm. God is so good–another "drink from His river of delights."

Jim did hit his head on a sign as we climbed up a little hill to get across from one parking lot to a street and it about knocked him out. He doesn't like hitting his head, not only because it hurts, but it leaves him with a scab on his beautiful "dome." It was so exhilarating to get to the bridge! What a glorious day in which we had our own celebration!

Worn out but gleeful!

Jim: Glenda was awesome! A fifteen-mile walk with a backpack on a warm day is no easy matter. What a trooper. She had said on the *Walk* there were times she wished she could walk with me some of the way. Today, she had her chance, seized it, and passed with flying colors. We were very, very tired at the close of the day, but she made it. I was so proud of her. What a tough woman! (And cute, too!)

Then we decided to take a bus back to the hotel. Walking fifteen miles was much easier than trying to decide which bus and route to take us back to our RV in Secaucus. However, we finally chose a bus, got on, and Glenda, sharing her frustration with the bus driver, began to question him about routes.

Glenda: I did get a little nervous. We had to get back to the RV and it was starting to get dark. I was afraid we might get fouled up with bus changes and get stuck in some questionable area, but God provided for us.

God always did provide, sometimes just in the nick of time, but that kept us looking to Him.

Jim: The driver was great in helping us, and went a step further by connecting us with someone he knew who was a regular bus passenger. The man, Edgar, a forty-one-year-old mechanic from El Salvador, took care of us by staying with us until our final connecting bus came to take us back to Secaucus. After we boarded our bus, he waved goodbye and walked to his bus. Our "nameless" bus driver and Edgar were two more angels we met on the *Walk* across America.

Surprise in New York City!

On Thursday, September 26, we took a taxi from the hotel to the Hudson Terrace, the base of the George Washington Bridge on the New Jersey side around 10:00 a.m. This was a trial ride in a taxi as part of our *MMM* preparation. We were trying to determine the best way to take our family from the hotel to the bridge on October 4. The Hudson Terrace was where our family would gather, and we would begin the walk across the bridge. Knowing the way by taxi saved us on October 4, as our taxi drivers got confused.

Made it to the George Washington Bridge

Glenda and I walked the bridge to simulate the family walk on October 4; we made it in thirty minutes. The day wasn't as clear as the day before, but still nice. We walked along the Hudson River, "checking things out" for the *Walk* in New York with family and friends. That day, Glenda and I had some disagreements and Glenda even had a meltdown, stemming from the complete physical and emotional exhaustion of the six-month trip across America.

This became a special time for us because Glenda shared her heart, letting go of many fears she carried and struggled with on the trip. These were fears for my safety.

Glenda: As we got into more hills, turns, and traffic, there were times that I would cry out to God–literally–for Jim's safety. I would watch as Jim would be going up a hill and, from where I was sitting, I could see speeding cars and semi-trucks coming over the hill–they could not see Jim nor could Jim see them. My mind would go to horrific scenarios–all the "what ifs." It didn't help that I had heard of others who had been killed that same year attempting to walk across America. So, I would reach out to Jim and cry to God, many times with tears streaming down my face, "Keep the drivers alert, keep Jim alert. **Protect him, Lord Jesus, protect him!**" Praise His Holy Name – HE DID!!

Jim: As she shared, I felt bad for her and for a while was not much, if any, help, but I listened and let her unload. Then, God softened both of our hearts. We shared our hurts, fears, and exhaustion. On the side of the Hudson River, we cried, hugged each other and prayed. It was a clearing of the air and that day brightened considerably.

That day was another testimony to the fact that the *Walk* was so similar to life. The day improved after sharing. As we added eating at Whole Foods near Central Park and having Jamba Juice for dessert, the day continued to improve.

We were "undercover" in New York City because "officially" the *Walk* had not yet reached New York City. "Undercover" meant I was not wearing my neon orange shirt with "I'm Walking Across America" on it. I was disguised in street clothes. While walking near Rockefeller Center, we ran into good friends, Paul and Linda Hagan, whom we know from working with them at the TCM mission in Austria. They were in New York City, waiting to go on a cruise.

They laughed and told us that they had just been talking about us, wondering, "Where are Jim and Glenda today?" Then, BOOM, we were there. All of us were surprised and laughed about the small world we live in and the chance of running into each other in the Big Apple. So cool! We visited for a few moments, then continued on with our separate journeys.

Glenda and I walked to Times Square, took the 320 bus to Walmart in Secaucus, and drove out to Kevin and Sherry's, arriving about 10:00 p.m. It was a long, but special day in New York, now ending being at "home" in Millstone Township at the McSweeney's. Oh, so nice to sleep in a regular bed. We were one day closer to our *MMM*.

Back "Home" at the McSweeney's for Rest

We loved being at Kevin and Sherry's home. They were so gracious to provide a place of comfort and relaxation for us. We slept in until 7:00 a.m. on Friday, September 27, and had a leisurely morning. During the day, we did some RV chores, then contacted Jared, who was attending a conference in San Francisco.

When Kevin came home from work, we played pool. I beat him in two games which never happens as he is light years better than I. Either the pain in his knees was so great (he was to have knee-replacement surgery on both knees soon), or he was just being a gracious host. Either way, we had fun.

He is a special man. (He had the surgery after our *Walk*, fought through the recovery, and now has two new knees.)

That evening, we had a great dinner with Kevin and Sherry, then saw his pictures from 9/11, as well as pictures of the George Washington Bridge that he oversees. These were fascinating to us as Kevin was very involved in the search for 9/11 victims, friends of his who were members of the Port Authority in New York and New Jersey. While all Americans were touched by 9/11, Kevin was more so as he knew and had worked with people who died that day.

Saturday, September 28, was such a relaxing day that I entered in my journal, *today was a leisurely day*. It was nice to be "back home" with Kevin and Sherry.

Brooklyn Tabernacle Service Launches the "Final Week"

On Sunday, September 29, we decided it would be a treat to visit the Brooklyn Tabernacle for church. It was a very good decision. Kevin was our driver and guide again, this time into Brooklyn. The drive continued our education, as we were able to see parts of greater New York City that we had not yet seen. We crossed many bridges, including the Brooklyn Bridge, and drove through parts of New York that had a countryside look. That was surprising. New York City is not all concrete jungle.

Finding the Brooklyn Tabernacle was not easy with many one-way streets, some extremely narrow. After backtracking due to some confusing directions from the GPS, we arrived at the church. We knew we were close by the crowd of people that were going to a very big and powerful church.

Making the trip to the church was well worth it. The Brooklyn Tabernacle meets in an old, beautiful theater. When we arrived, only a few of the 3,200 seats were empty. We found four together and squeezed in before the singing and praise began. Once we sat down, we noticed the choir loft was filled with nearly 300 people. The church is known for its choir, and we anticipated a great morning of music. We were not disappointed.

First, however, we met the people around us. I met an eighty-year-old woman next to me and informed her that I had walked from California to New York City to attend her church that day. She was stunned and quickly told her friends, who were buzzing with excitement, so I gave them brochures about the *Walk*.

As we talked and visited with people, the buzzing in the church was overshadowed by the praise music that began. The congregation stood and the singing began. It was the best singing I have ever heard in a church. The entire church actually sounded like a choir of over 3,500 people praising Jesus. The world famous Brooklyn Tabernacle Choir did sing a special number and lived up to their reputation, but I'll never forget the entire-church "choir" singing.

Pastor Jim Cymbala's message was from the Acts 15 story of Paul and Barnabas and how they handled a problem. Pastor Cymbala's message was clear.

We need to give people a second chance, because we all might need a second chance sometime.

It was a great Sunday, capped by a return "home" to relax and prepare for the final week of the *Walk*. We rested on Sunday afternoon, but were excited about the week ahead which would be the culmination of six months of walking across America. We were on the eve of our *Most Memorable Moment.*

Glenda's Glimpses: Second Chances

I certainly needed many second chances on the *Walk*. It was hard going day after day after day, with less-than-needed sleep. It was difficult coming to an agreeable solution on decisions we had to make. It wasn't easy for us to share and "move around" in a floor space of about 2 ½ x 8 feet. So, there were times that I needed a second chance. I could get grumpy and disagreeable. I wasn't always lovable. It's true that I never complained about rubbing Jim's feet at noon and night–on the outside. But there were times that my thoughts grumbled. I'm sure it leaked out to my countenance, but Jim was willing to give me second chances. Thank you, Jim, for your grace.

REFLECTIONS ON WEEK 26

We often felt that the Walk was a lot like life.

God always went before us and was always with us.

*God always provided—sometimes just in the nick of time
—but that kept us looking to Him.*

We need to give people a second chance—we all might need one sometime.

****

*Bear with each other and forgive whatever grievances you may have against
one another. Forgive as the Lord forgave you.*
(Colossians 3:13)

Week 27

Sept 30 - October 4 – Secaucus, NJ to New York City, NY
10 Miles to the Finish

Victory Walk

The Final Week Begins! Exciting!

The time had come for the "final week" of the *Walk*. Anticipating a fantastic week, it was time to go to work.

On Monday, September 30, we left McSweeney's around 1:00 p.m., arriving in Secaucus about 2:30 p.m. Since the hotel was not ready for us until Tuesday, we parked at Walmart. We took the bus to Union City to scout out how long it would take for the family to take the bus to Fort Lee on Friday.

After over two hours and several bus exchanges, we ruled out taking the bus. Yes, bus transportation would save us some money, but the ordeal of getting on and off busses with strollers, infants, and small children would not be worth the savings. Our family's safety and peace of mind are more important than money. Friday, October 4, was our day to walk with our family across the George Washington Bridge.

We decided to take taxis from the hotel to Fort Lee to walk across the bridge, then walk to Times Square. It would be a mile across the bridge, then nine more miles to Times Square. It would be a lengthy walk for everyone, but would conclude the *Walk*. At Times Square, we planned to celebrate.

After deciding on taxis, Glenda and I walked the George Washington Bridge to New York City, took busses and subways to 57th street where we planned to pick up tickets for *Wicked* for Tuesday night, October 1. I wanted to treat Glenda to something special in New York City as a small thank you for her gallant effort of accompanying me and providing all I needed to walk across America. She was thrilled with the gift. I was thrilled that she was with me the whole *Walk*.

Friends from Newbury Park, Tom and Diane Maronde, were in New York on their way to a cruise to enjoy the beautiful fall colors of New England. Talking with them by phone and sharing the plan to get tickets, they said they would buy them to hold for us since their hotel was right next to the theater. They secured them, and we picked up the tickets at the ticket office Monday evening. With the tickets in our hands, we went to eat at a Thai restaurant on Broadway.

Tom and Diane had already eaten, but met us at the restaurant. When we tried to pay for the tickets, they refused to take our money and said it was their gift to us. Emotionally humbled and deeply grateful, we simply said, "Thank you." Having friends like that is so awesome. They are favorite people of ours and have been so generous and so good to us through the years in many ways. We had a marvelous time with them.

That night, reflecting on our time with the Marondes and their gift to us, I simply wrote in my journal, *So cool!*

Getting to bed at 11:40 p.m., I also wrote in my journal, *Glenda is shot... soooo tired.*

"Wicked" Musical – An Evening with Two Glendas

We really enjoyed *Wicked,* an exciting Broadway musical. Glenda had a special reason for enjoying it since her name is the same as the star of the show–Glenda, the Good Witch. We didn't get to bed until 1:30 a.m., but it was a special day!

Glenda: What a treat! Thank you, Jim. Thank you, Tom and Diane.

Glenda's Glimpses: Arrivals

Our family arrived in Secaucus on Wednesday and Thursday, October 2 and 3, in time for the bridge crossing on October 4. Arrival times were busy. Having decided earlier that the RV would not make a good shuttle vehicle from Newark Airport to the hotel, each family took taxis, and it worked out fine.

Jim: Jason had the biggest family and hired a man named Ralph to transport him in a large SUV. That worked out well, because Ralph *just happened* to oversee a taxi fleet. We secured him to arrange transportation from the hotel to Fort Lee on Friday morning, October 4.

Glenda: There was only one hitch with the whole family. A taxi driver took Jared, Steph, Fayth, and Stephen to the wrong Extended Stay. There were three Extended Stay Hotels in the area, and those two were just 2-3 miles apart; but they had to get another cab to take them there since their cab had left and it was too far to walk, pulling luggage and pushing strollers. That's pretty good with all the families and friends arriving to have only one mishap.

Jim: Several friends were also arriving, several staying at the Extended Stay Hotel with us. Others had secured lodging in different places, but all these friends were the ones who would gather on the New York side of the George Washington Bridge to welcome the Buckley family as we were exiting the bridge.

Excitement was building. Glenda and I rejoiced that all twenty-five of our Buckley family had arrived safely and were excited about joining the last part of the *Walk* across America. It was a dream come true. Our *MMM* was close!

Glenda's Glimpses: Mom/Grandma Hat

As usual, I had my "mom/grandma" hat on as everyone arrived. I was bustling around, making sure everyone had what they needed. I checked to see who wanted to take a trip to Walmart to buy food. We needed to think through who would ride in which cabs, which families we could combine, which ones needed to ride in a vehicle with room for strollers, diaper bags. My mind was whirling and my feet weren't far behind! Moms are forever moms.

Jim: The night before the October 4 walk, I gathered all of our family and friends staying at the hotel for a briefing. After my final instructions, our twins, Jamye and Jared, closed us in a powerful prayer time. I think everyone in the room was moved! I could hardly wait for the morning when we would do what I had dreamed about for months. Our *Most Memorable Moment* was close! The plan to walk the bridge with family, meet friends, and walk the Hudson River to Times Square would be the conclusion of the *Walk* across America. It would be our "Victory Walk."

Introducing Our Most Memorable Moment

Writing about the *Walk* for the past several months has been exciting. Remembering the trip in its entirety has been refreshing. Using transcripts from my recorder and entries in my daily journal, I had too much material. We reduced and reduced.

With information from Glenda's Glimpses and her prayer letters, she had too much material. As novice writers, our biggest problem was trying to decide which information not to include. (I think we edited out an entire book.)

Preparing to write about the final day and our *MMM*, I'm at a loss for words. I'm tempted to say, "We walked the bridge, saw friends, ate, walked the Hudson River to Times Square, hugged, took the bus back to Secaucus, and had pizza." That's what happened.

However, there are details of that final walk that would fill pages—certainly filled our hearts to overflowing. As I look at that final day, I get emotional. There were fireworks going off inside me where words seem inadequate, but we will use words to share some of the fireworks.

How do I summarize the final moments of a 187-day, 3,131-mile *Walk?* I averaged 22.1 miles a day, faced enormous challenges, walked through seventeen states, and touched thousands of lives in homes, on the road, on Facebook, and through media. Words fail me.

How can Glenda summarize driving an RV 9,000 miles across America, "a half a mile at a time"? She faithfully rubbed my feet twice daily, prepared six months of meals in an RV, and prayed as she watched me walk, afraid I was going to be killed by a truck coming around a blind curve. She got two hours less sleep a night than she needs, missed being available to help with two new grandbabies, missed being home with family on Mother's Day, her birthday, and July 4. Words fail her.

Convinced that the best I can do is break the day into parts, there will be four parts in sharing our *Most Memorable Moment.* In each part, there will be facts, but Glenda and I will share our hearts, which were deeply touched by our *Most Memorable Moment*–the final day of the *Walk*.

Microcosm of our Family Goal–Fifty Years Ago!

The final day was a culmination of the *Walk*, but also a microcosm of our family goal, our dream life together, that began on a walk in Eugene, Oregon, forty-eight years ago. It was a walk through life that we believe and pray will take our family to heaven, plus many others we meet along the way.

I pray you enjoy the final walk of the *Walk* across America. For Glenda and me, it was a "short" ten-mile walk that represented our lifelong walk with Jesus. The 187-day *Walk* and the ten-mile *Walk* on October 4 have changed my life forever. My prayer is that everyone who experiences the final *Walk* and our *MMM* with us in the next few pages will be changed by Jesus as well.

MMM #1: The Family Gathered

October 4, 2013, day 187, was the final day of the *Walk* across America. We ate early to feed the kids and prepare for the ten-mile walk to Times Square. At 8:30 a.m., we gathered to get everyone into the four separate vans and cars needed to transport us to the Hudson Terrace area in Fort Lee, the New Jersey entrance to the bridge.

Sixteen friends had already left to travel by rapid transit to meet our family on the New York City side of the George Washington Bridge as we exited. They also picked up food so everyone could eat an early lunch. Many of these friends had already risen early to be on the TODAY show on Thursday to announce, "Pastor Jim Buckley has walked across America." Awesome friends!

Gathering at the bridge entrance at Fort Lee took some extra time as three of the vehicle drivers weren't sure of the exact location. After some cell phone calls to direct confused drivers, everyone arrived at the correct spot. We were very excited to be together for the beginning of the day's walk.

Buckley family ready to cross the George Washington Bridge

The BGEA Team, led by Kevin Adamson, met us at the bridge. The family posed for some pictures and the beginning of the video filming. A strong spirit of nervousness, fulfillment, and excitement filled the entire family, from the little to the big. I gave the family some final instructions and a "pep talk." This was it. I was stoked inside, with excitement racing all through me.

Over 3,100 miles had been walked across America. We were ready to walk the final ten miles to Times Square, starting with the bridge. Although overflowing with joy, excitement, and wanting to jump up and down, I resisted as I knew I had to maintain my "game face." We had a huge day ahead of us. Ten miles is no easy walk for some of our family, as well as for some of our friends joining us in New York, then walking with us to Times Square. A time for celebrating was coming!

Before we walked the bridge, Glenda gave all twenty-five of us a picture of Ryan's grave site and a story of the article I wrote about Jeremy–we carried memories of two Buckley's that were already home in heaven. Then twenty-five of us prepared to walk or ride in strollers across the bridge. Essentially that day, a total of twenty-seven of us were crossing the bridge as one united family.

The first part of our **Most Memorable Moment** was in process. The family gathered to walk the bridge. We delayed a few minutes, as Jared loaded a message to send to Facebook to send right as we began crossing the bridge. After we prayed, we walked.

MMM #2: The Family Walked the Bridge

At 10:20 a.m., we walked as one unit, with the neon orange shirts, with strollers, and with flashing lights to keep us protected from bikers zipping across the bridge. Glenda and I walked in the lead, with the BGEA Team ahead, beside, and behind us as we walked, getting all kinds of video footage. My heart was pounding with all kinds of emotion.

This bridge walk represented so much.

The bridge walk launched the final part of the *Walk*. It represented the goal that Glenda and I had set for our family when we married–when we were just a family of two. Simply stated, our family goal was to get our entire family to heaven. (In my mind, walking the bridge was symbolic to walking into heaven.) On this day, we had twenty-five walking. Tears came to my eyes. I want nothing more in life than the end of life to be just like today, our family walking into heaven. We know we'll go at different times as two are already there. That thought brought tears. As I walked, I had flash thoughts about Jeremy, our son in heaven, and Ryan, our grandson who's already with his uncle. I remembered the heartache of losing a child. I remembered the brokenness of losing a grandson and watching our son and daughter-in-law in brokenness. They were with us on the bridge, not talking, but feeling.

It was a nice day for a walk, with a slight overcast. Although I could write pages about my feelings, the walk across the bridge only took thirty minutes and was fun. Glenda suggested that family members take turns coming to the front to walk and talk with me as we were being videoed by the BGEA Team. That was special and added to my emotions.

Walking with auto and truck traffic to our left and the railing over the Hudson River to our right, we made good time. The little ones were in strollers and that was a good idea. We had two flashing safety lights at the rear to caution bicyclers to slow down. They did. We didn't need safety flashers in the front, as the BGEA Team was there, and that slowed oncoming walkers and bicyclers.

The bridge crossing was even more than I anticipated. It was a walk that reminded Glenda and me of our family goal. It was a unifying walk for our family, as we shared our family goal once again before the walk. It was a statement that **this family belongs to Jesus.** We stated that goal when we were married in 1968 and have never wavered in our commitment. In fact, we are committed to it now more than ever.

Tears flooded my eyes as we walked the bridge. Like all homes and families, ours has been, and will continue to be, tested and challenged. Satan doesn't want Jesus in our homes; but Jesus has been the difference maker in our home, bringing us victory through times of battles, challenges, and conflicts. We are far from a perfect family, but we love Jesus. Glenda and I pray nightly on our knees for Jesus to be in every home and life in our family. With those thoughts in my mind for six months of walking, this bridge walk was a statement of victory in Jesus and defiance against Satan.

As we neared the end of the bridge, tears flooded my eyes. In my heart and mind, I silently shouted to the world, "**This family belongs to Jesus! We are on our way to heaven!**" Jesus lives in our hearts and homes, and we want that for every home in this nation and world.

At home, after the *Walk,* I had breakfast at home with two friends, Tom Stephen and Tim Smith. Both spoke highly of the picture of the end of the bridge walk, saying that it was a landmark picture of the *Walk.* It's a picture of a family legacy. Our youngest son wrote a Facebook entry entitled, "*Leaving* or *Living* a Legacy?"

My two friends at breakfast said, "That's what people want–a family together. They want to know what you did and how you built a family like this that walks together with Jesus."

Coming off the George Washington Bridge

It was 10:50 a.m. when we saw the end of the bridge and walked down a sloping curve, waving to the sixteen cheering friends gathered there to greet us.

Greeted by friends

It was a glorious walk on an incredible day. Yes! It was definitely a *Most Memorable Moment* of the *Walk*. I can honestly say that the bridge crossing was far more than I anticipated it being. I loved every one of those precious thirty minutes.

At the grassy area on the New York side of the bridge, we hugged, filmed, visited, then ate a bite before continuing our journey down the Hudson toward Times Square.

Glenda's Glimpses: Awesome Sight and Feeling

It was such an awesome sight and feeling as I looked back to see all those orange shirts, but it was more awesome to look at the faces of those we love so much. Then to see those cheering for us, holding signs as we came around and down off the bridge made my heart swell. It still does each time I see the picture taken of us coming down the walkway single file off the George Washington Bridge.

MMM #3: Family and Friends Walk to Times Square

Special Note: The walk down the Hudson River, then crossing into Central Park, on to Broadway, and finally to Times Square took about four hours. We visited with people along the way who saw the forty-one orange shirts coming their way with shirts that read:

God said GO...So he Went!
My Dad Walked Across America
My Grandad Walked Across America
My Husband Walked Across America
I (Jesus) Walked Across America

Glenda's Glimpses: Where's Jim?

When Jim would be more towards the back of the orange shirts, people we met would say, "Who is Dad?" Or "Who is Grandad?" Inevitably, when they reached Jim, they would stop, shake his hand, and some would chat with him.

As we headed down towards Times Square, Jim was less and less in the lead. Someone in our group would say, "Where's Jim?" We would look back and he would be talking to someone. It was not unusual for Jim. As much as he is a stickler about "staying on schedule," whenever he would stop to talk to someone on the road, time stood still for him. He has a way of so quickly connecting with people. He makes them feel important, like a friend. My personal opinion is that is why God chose Jim to do this—he is so focused on making distance, but also focused on the people he meets.

Jim: At times I did stop to talk with people, but encouraged my team to keep walking. I would catch them. One time when I was lagging behind the group after talking, a man on a bicycle rode by and said to me, "Hi Grandad." He had been seeing the grandkids' shirts and seemed pleased with himself that he found "Grandad." It proved also that people were reading the other shirts, whether they stopped and talked or not.

We walked and talked, stopping at times to rest. It was a long walk. We met so many people, stopping to talk with many of them. However, we had to keep walking to make it to Times Square.

I met a couple at a stop light and talked for less than a minute. She was a nutritionist who asked me three quick questions.

"What was your favorite drink on the *Walk*?"

"Water, by far."

"Did you drink any coconut water?"

"As much as I could find."

"Did you drink Gatorade?"

"No. Too much sugar. Preferred water."

It was my first exam on the *Walk*.

Smiling, she said, "You passed."

Later, I met a man named Joseph. He was very enthusiastic and thrilled about the *Walk*. An African-American, probably in his sixties, he told me that he could never do that.

I said, "You just do one step at a time."

He smiled.

I said, "Joseph is a Bible name."

He grinned, adding that he knew the story of Joseph in the Bible as this Joseph was a Bible man.

Following is an **"excerpt"** from my recorder that I still was using on that final day:

We're close to the area of the Hudson River where the heroic pilot landed the plane with nobody being killed in that accident. We have two guys in front of us, Eric and Kevin. They're the photographer and the producer of the video, and they turn and take pictures of us occasionally, and they are filming me walking and talking.

As they were filming me and those with me at 1:30 in the afternoon, I was walking with two of my grandchildren; Joshua, twelve, was on my left, and, Abby, twelve, was on my right. These are two of thirteen very special people in my life. (Following is a conversation directed to the camera.)

Jim: "So, it has been a great day. We're over halfway to Times Square from the bridge. The bridge walk was super. Abby loved it, didn't you?"

Abby: "Yes," smiling.

Jim: "Joshua loved it, didn't you?"

Joshua: "Yeah!" smiling.

Jim: "So, that goes on the record. It was fun. Did the bouncing of the bridge bother you, Abby?"

Abby: "No."

Jim: "It did bounce. Did you feel it, Joshua?"

Joshua: "Not really."

I enjoyed walking and talking with family and friends as we made our way to Times Square.

Along the Hudson River

Glenda's Glimpses: Passing the Baton

So much happened on the nine miles from the George Washington Bridge to Times Square. Our grandkids were busy handing out our "Walking Across America" brochures and cards to people. We walked along the Hudson, then turned inland, landing in Central Park where our *oldest* grandson, Jordan, interestingly led the way. Symbolic of "passing the baton"?

Through Central Park

MMM #4: At Times Square We Celebrated the Walk

At 3:47, we arrived at Times Square–what a glorious day! I don't know how to even summarize in words the feelings that I had rushing and racing through me that day at Times Square when Glenda and I walked in.

Glenda's Glimpses: God's Hand

As we stepped into Times Square, there were flashes of something right in front of us. As the person photographing us lowered his camera down, we recognized him as someone from home, Jeff Vaillancourt, who just happened to be in New York.

I later emailed him, "It's amazing how God orchestrated things—you in New York when we were."

Jeff's picture of us walking into Times Square

Jeff answered, "So true. I wasn't even working in New York City, I was just flying out of JFK and had a couple hours to kill. I parked, walked out in the middle of Times Square, waited a few minutes, and there you all came. It was truly amazing. It was a blessing and clearly God had His hand in it. I'm so thankful."

Jim: All I knew was that I wanted to be walking in holding Glenda's hand. We walked in hand-in-hand. We started dating hand-in-hand, and that's what we've done through the years.

Glenda: Little did we know that our **first walk** in October of 1965, would someday lead us to this glorious moment of walking into Times Square hand-in-hand to celebrate a 3,131-mile walk across America, forty-eight years later.

Jim: Into Times Square we walked, the love of my life by my side, and the Champion of the *Walk*, Jesus, right with us. The three of us entered Times Square. I told Glenda before we arrived there that this was not my victory, this was our victory. She had fought the challenges with me all the way. Every woman in this country, every woman in this world, will be able to rethink the whole idea of surrender as they read Glenda's Glimpses. Glenda is a very strong woman, but she has surrendered and walked by my side, been by my side–she has been my everything. We are a team!

So, I told her, "I'm going to grab your hand and we are going to raise our hands in victory together."

Well, I tried to do that, but one hand of each of us together wasn't enough. So, we faced each other, grabbed both hands and raised hands together. Once that happened, we instantly hugged and cried, tears of relief, joy, and victory!

It was just a fantastic and joyous moment, the moment of a lifetime. Later, I watched us on the Times Square web camera for the whole world to see. I had heard someone mention a camera, but didn't think about it again until our good friend, Edgard Mello, phoned me and said he could see us at Times Square.

When I asked him where he was, he said, "Brazil. I'm watching you on the Times Square Webcam. Congratulations!"

Wow! The whole world could see. Guess that's why the Lord led us to Times Square. Awesome!

Glenda and I hugged and then held hands. We didn't say much at first. Words were not adequate. What was the feeling I had at the end of the *Walk*? Overwhelmed and thankful.

Sometime later Glenda and I kissed, and I remember saying to her, **"We made it! The *Walk* is over!"**

She told me, "I'm so proud of you."

I teared some more.

Our son, Jared, with tears of joy and excitement, shouted to the crowd in his resounding voice, "Ladies and gentleman. This man has just finished walking across America."

There was applause from those who heard him. Meanwhile, the BGEA Team was filming all of this.

Looking back, I wonder what it looked like to the people visiting Times Square. Forty-one people in orange shirts arrived at Times Square with cameramen filming every move. Times Square, famous for celebrity moments, may have moments like this quite often. However, when we formed the orange prayer circle and I prayed a prayer of celebration and thanksgiving, that might have been different from others types of celebration moments.

All the above happened in moments, but fireworks of emotion raced inside me. I was relieved that we had made it. I was ecstatic that the call from Jesus to *Walk* across America had been obeyed.

Simple obedience is highly underrated.

I felt His approval. Glenda and I then began hugging and thanking every family member and friend who had supported, prayed, worked with us, and walked with us to Times Square.

Glenda's Glimpses: Who?

I remember relief. We were safe. We made it. We were done! No one could take that from us.

I was so proud of Jim. I watched him walk across deserts, walk over hills and mountains, walk across plains, walk through farmland, walk by marshes, walk across bridges, walk around corners, walk past cars and trucks, walk on narrow roads with even narrower shoulders, walk on wide divided highways with broad shoulders, walk through grass with ticks, walk through city streets, and walk on small-town sidewalks. I saw him stop to talk to people. I saw him walk in the rain, in 100-degree weather, and in sixty-mile-an-hour wind. I watched him get up very early, taking off as soon as the sun was up, going to bed well after the sun went down. I saw him reading his Bible daily, writing in his journal, and writing emails late into the night.

Who is this man? He is a fully devoted man of God, disciplined, and determined to the core. He is well-liked by those he meets for a few minutes and those he has known for years. Who is this man? He's the dedicated father of my children, the attentive, fun-loving grandfather of our grandkids, my devoted and loving husband, and the love of my life. James Dean Buckley, I love you so, and am so proud of you!

Walk? Someday we will walk across that bridge on our final walk. But for now, we will continue to walk hand-in-hand, the Lord Jesus right here with us.

So, Jim, when you say, "I think God wants me to...."

I'll say, "Can I go?"

On Red Stairs at Father Duffy Square

Some closing statements from my recorder:

It is 5:20 on October 4, and we are now leaving Times Square, headed to the bus station. The Walk is over. My legs are shot. I'm tired from standing. I am anxious to get on a bus and get back to the hotel, have a celebration, thank everybody, thank Jesus, and reflect a little bit, let others reflect, then have a prayer and praise time, and go to sleep. That sounds so good.

Glenda's Glimpses: Names

Our son, Daniel, and the grandkids had prepared a special song. It was fun. It was nice to be able to sit and relax. The hotel let us take over the courtyard. The "cousins" played with their "adopted cousins," Scott, Carsten, and Emori Wurth. Besides relaxing, playing, and eating, different ones shared their thoughts about the day, the *Walk*. Among those who shared were our Lead Pastor, Ken LaMont; chairman of our elder board, Mark Bodenhamer; and Coordinator of the *Walk*, Leslie Haggard; and of course, our kids.

Emotions were still running high. Todd and Kristi Wurth, flew in from Wyoming; John and Pat Bailey, (mother of our daughter-in-law, Brigett), from Texas; friends Bob and Susie Zweigler, Ken and Brenda LaMont, Leslie Haggard, Mark Bodenhamer, and Lynda Gutierrez, all from Newbury Park; and Lynda's son, Nicky Gutierrez, from Denver; while Brandi Campbell drove up from Maryland. Sounds like a list from the Old Testament, but just as all those names meant something to people back then, these people mean something to us.

The list that means most to us reads like this:

Son, Andrew and wife Cheryl Buckley, Abby 12 (at the time), Aaron, 10;

Son, Jason and Brigett Buckley, Jordan, 13, Joshua, 12, Jacob, 11, Jadyn, 10, Jeremy, almost 3;

Son, Daniel and Charity Buckley, Mikaela, 9, Gabby, 5;

Daughter, Jamye and Robert Sack, Emma, 3, Shyloh, 7 months;

Son, Jared and Stephanie Buckley, Fayth, 4, Stephen, 7 ½ months.

Again, it's a list of names to you, but each one has a special place in our hearts and prayers. They are joined by Noah and Journey, born since that day, and by Jeremy Stephen and Ryan Stephen, who have already crossed that final bridge. Twenty-nine in all.

One of the things that I said early on the *Walk* was that we have given permission to our kids and grandkids (spouses included) to do crazy things. Our daughter-in-law, Brigett, said we have sent a message to each of them to do whatever God calls them to do.

Who knows what our kids and grandkids will accomplish by saying, "Yes," to God? Who knows what can happen for the Kingdom if we all, you included, say, "Yes," to God?

This *Walk* is over, but Jesus is not done.

Thanks be to God! He gives us the victory through our Lord Jesus Christ.
(1 Corinthians 15:57)

Family in New York
October 5-6

Ground Zero, Ferry, Manhattan – October 5, 2013

Saturday, October 5, was the day after the *Walk* across America was finished and the call from the Lord was obeyed. However, Inviting America Home was not finished and won't be until every home has Jesus living in it. *(You can read more about this in the Epilogue.)* Saturday, for the Buckley family, was a day for seeing the sights and having fun in New York City.

We took a ferry ride by the Statue of Liberty (closed while we were there) to Staten Island and back to Manhattan where we ate. After that, we visited Ground Zero–very touching. We walked Manhattan some before returning to Secaucus. It was a fun day, with us walking "only" nine miles.

Bus Ride to Hillsong Church

On Sunday, October 6, our family decided to attend Hillsong NYC, a dynamic church in Manhattan. We all decided to wear our orange shirts that day.

We met our bus driver that morning, Arturo, who took us into New York. He watched as a lot of excited and wiggly orange shirts boarded his bus. When we arrived in New York, Glenda and I visited with Arturo while we waited to be last off the bus.

Glenda to Arturo: **"Do you want to know who you just brought to New York?"**

Arturo: "Yes."

Glenda: **"You brought the family of a man who just walked across America,"** pointing to me (Jim) as she spoke. **"My husband walked across America...."**

Jim: **"It was for Jesus."**

Arturo: "Oh, it's Christian. It's so good. My wife became a Christian just recently. I don't know how this is going to work."

Jim: **"Are you a believer?"**

Arturo: "Oh, yes, I'm a believer in Jesus all my life, but it's a new thing for our home."

Jim: **"Make sure you have Jesus live in your home."**

Pointing to the orange shirts getting off the bus, I continued.

Jim: **"This is what can happen if you make Jesus #1 in your home, as my wife and I did forty-five years ago. He has made the difference."**

Arturo: "Oh, this is wonderful, this is wonderful."

I could just sense what he was seeing and thinking. Orange will be his reminder that Jesus is at work in a home. What a word of hope from the Lord for Arturo.

ORANGE Hits the Streets in New York City on October 6

Having the entire family walking in **orange shirts** through the streets of New York City on Sunday was unforgettable. People stopped, asked questions. The story below is what happened after church as we walked to Rockefeller Center down Fifth Avenue during a Polish Parade. It was awesome for the entire family to see what an impact a united and focused family can make in a world where families and homes are so shattered. The family was amazing, stopping and talking with people who wanted to know "what was going on" with the shirts, not the parade.

On the walk that Sunday, I met an auxiliary police officer named Chris, who saw on my shirt that I had walked across America. Following is our brief conversation. Due to her breathing difficulties, her statements and questions were short. Chris in *italics*.

Is that real?

Yes, it is. I started in California and came to New York.

Why'd you walk?

Jesus said to.

That makes sense. American homes need hope. We're going down the tubes.

Well, the hope we found has been in Jesus living in every heart and home.

That's it. If we don't have that, we have no hope at all. That's our only hope.

Chris was a police officer on September 11, 2001, and worked at Ground Zero for the next twenty-three days. Twelve years later, she's sick with breathing problems, most likely related to 9/11. After the horror of that day had calmed some, she told me she talked with several survivors who told her what they were thinking as they were fleeing for their lives.

They wanted two things:

#1– get home to family,

#2– have peace.

When life falls apart or is ending, priorities rise to the top—home and peace. Nobody said they wanted a better job, nicer car, bigger home or more money. They wanted home and peace. That was what the *Walk* was all about. Jesus provides a home and a life with peace.

It was a fascinating visit with Chris. I told her I would be praying for her. What does she need? What does America need?

Peace at home that only comes from Jesus.

Epilogue
January 14, 2015

Yes, I walked across America in obedience to a call from Jesus, but I still can't get one of the messages of the *Walk* out of my mind. It came late in the afternoon, somewhere in the Midwest.

Jim, as important as the Walk is, what is more important is what happens after the Walk.

Since I wasn't sure what that meant at the time, I filed it for "after the *Walk*."

At the church in Brooklyn, we sang "Christ alone, Cornerstone, the weak made strong by the Savior's love..." and tears rolled down my cheeks. I knew I was weak, Jesus was strong, and He made the *Walk* happen. I walked with Him. At times He carried me. I was humbled. All I did was obediently walk with Jesus, one step at a time.

The next Sunday at Hillsong Church, we sang the same song. Tears again, but this time, I said to the Lord, "I got the message last week. You are strong and I am weak."

As the singing continued, I heard more, "It's time to be obedient after the *Walk*. You will need Me more after the *Walk* than during the *Walk* because this next step may be harder. Remember, the weak made strong by the Savior's love. Jim, you are weak, but I am strong. Together, we will make the next step happen."

We left for home after the *Walk* and life continued.

That was October 6, 2013. In early 2014, I started writing little reminders of the *Walk,* one week at a time. Writing memories weekly for twenty-seven weeks, I concluded writing in July of 2014. Glenda and I started checking on what it would take to make the writings into a book. We were in no hurry until one day, on our way to share the story of the *Walk* with eighty seniors, a song flashed in my mind. It was from a great hymn:

We've a story to tell to the nations,
That shall turn their hearts to the right.
A story of truth and mercy,
A story of peace and light....

Jim, it's time to tell the story. Write the book!

When I told Glenda I believed the Lord was telling me to write a book about the *Walk* she responded, "Can I help?" (Sound familiar?)

Absolutely. Together we have written and are publishing the story of the *Walk* to help the message of the *Walk* reach every life and every home in America. That's His mission, and we are the messengers.

Jesus wants to live in every heart and home. It's time to take that story and message, now in a book, to the world. The *Walk* across America is not over, it may be just the beginning.

I pray that as you read the story of the *Walk,* you ask, "Can I go?"

The answer is, "Absolutely!"

Let's go together, one heart, one home at a time, and share with every person and every home that Jesus wants to live and walk with them daily. How do we do such a task?

Read this book. Give one to a friend.

But first, invite Jesus into your heart. Invite Him into your home. Walk with Him daily.

One life, one home at a time will be the start of the long-awaited revival to sweep across this great nation. Jesus will bring hope to every life and every home in America.

Today America. Tomorrow the world.

Jesus is ready! Glenda and I are ready!

It's time! Let's go.

Authors' Page

J im and Glenda Buckley were raised on farms and in Christian homes – Jim in California and Glenda in Oregon. They met at Northwest Christian College in Eugene, Oregon and dated for three years before marriage in 1968. Their life of marriage and family has paralleled their life of ministry.

Together they have five children who married and brought fifteen grandchildren into the Buckley family.

Together they have ministered in five different churches in three states. Jim and Glenda have been in Newbury Park, California, at the Newbury Park First Christian Church since 1983, serving for twenty-eight years as Lead Pastor and the past four years as Teaching Pastor.

Glenda has ministered by Jim's side while being a wife and mother. She has supported and participated in Jim's ministry in various ways, but excels in teaching women and using her musical gifts to bless lives. They have enjoyed sharing the challenges and joys of biblical marriage and family while leading marriage classes for over thirty years in Newbury Park. They have ministered **together** for forty-seven years.

Glenda helped carry extra loads while Jim was pursuing graduate education at Gordon-Conwell Theological Seminary in Massachusetts, receiving an M.T.S. degree and at Fuller Theological Seminary in Pasadena, California, receiving a D. Min. degree. In essence, they went to school **together.**

When Jim teaches at TCM International Institute in Austria, they serve **together** as Glenda serves as a short-term-worker at the graduate seminary.

When Jim heard God's call to walk across America, Glenda said, "Can I go?" **Together** they touched hearts and homes across America in 2013.

In *Walking Across America*, they **together** tell the life-changing story of walking across America **together!**

Their life **together** was established with Jesus being #1 in each of their lives and thus in their marriage and home. For them, **together** means not two, but three, as Jesus has been with them "every step of the way" along the walk of life.

In forty-seven years of marriage, family, and ministry, they have laughed, cried, served, struggled, traveled, prayed, sung, and dreamed **together**. In *Walking Across America, One Step at a Time*, they share **together** their dream and hope of Jesus living in every heart and home in America.

Appendix A
People Who Were "Crazy Enough" to Simply Obey God!

I knew some people thought I was "crazy" to walk across America. As I thought about it, I realized that there have been many before me that have done crazy things including Bible heroes like Noah, Abraham, Moses, David, and so many others. They obeyed God even when it seemed "crazy" to do so. These "crazy people" are listed in the Bible's "hall of faith" in Hebrews 11.

God's Hall of Faith of people in the Bible who obeyed God "by faith."

(All would have been called "crazy" to do so, but they did it.)

Noah built an ark to save his family. (Hebrews 11:7)

Abraham went to a new land without knowing where he was going. (Hebrews 11:8-10)

Abraham had a child at an old age. (Hebrews 11:11-12)

Moses' parents hid him to spare his life. (Hebrews 11:23)

Moses led hundreds of thousands out of bondage. (Hebrews 11:24-29)

Rahab welcomed the spies. (Hebrews 11:31)

Gideon led his "army" of 300 and defeated 120,000 Midianite swordsmen. (Hebrews 11:33; Judges 7:17-8:12)

David, as a shepherd boy, defeated a giant. (I Samuel 17:45-50, Hebrews 11:32)

These and so many others not named in Hebrews 11 were faithful throughout the Bible, doing what God said to do. They acted in faith and were "crazy" (in the eyes of the world) to do so.

As I further thought about it, I remembered my Grandad Buckley as a man who lived by faith, obeying God. He was "crazy" enough to trust God, even when facing death. Grandad could have fun in his closing hours and even laugh at his leaving this life. How could he do that? By faith, he knew he was going to heaven. Non-believers would call him "crazy." However, all the others listed above would have and probably were called "crazy" by the same non-believers. Yet, the "crazies" above changed the course of history by just being obedient.

Simple obedience is highly underrated!

All I was going to do was to walk across America. It was simply an act of obedience to bring hope to the homes of America. Yes. Some thought I was crazy. Some of my friends questioned whether I had heard God or not. However, I believed and I walked. What God did and will do in the future with that walk is up to Him. My job was to obey. I did. Yes. I would do it again if He called me to do it again.

How did I know? I asked three questions. If "yes" on all three, I believe it's God calling.

1. Does the Bible say not to do this or will this action be consistent with the Bible?
2. Would God be glorified in this act?

3. Will what I do help people to see God, be saved, and to draw closer to Him?

Is God calling you to do something "crazy" for Him? If so, you won't be the first or the last to simply obey. Do it and walk with a host of other "crazies" who dared to obey and change the course of lives and history.

Appendix B
Rules for the *Walk*

Before the *Walk* began, we made many preparations such as **Rules for the *Walk*** that were established for safety as walking across America can be very dangerous. These rules were established for my safety, as well as for the people wanting to walk with me.

The rules were as follows:

1. Wear a bright color so I could be seen. Shirts, jackets, and sweatshirts that I wore were all neon orange.
2. I generally walked into oncoming traffic so I could see vehicles coming toward me.
3. No walking in the dark (or even dusk, a dangerous time to be walking with the sun to my back, blinding drivers coming towards me.)
4. No walking during a lightning storm.
5. No walking on Sunday. We needed a day to rest and worship with Christians.
6. Walk alone on the open road.
7. May walk with one person on the open road in special situations.
8. In a town or a city, people may walk with me. This happened in Newbury Park, Phoenix, Washington, D.C., New York City, and a few other places.

9. I chose not to listen to music or recordings as I might be distracted from seeing traffic. I did talk on the phone, but had a blue tooth so my hands were free to walk using my walking sticks. I did talk into my cassette recorder on occasion, but always watching traffic as I talked.

Appendix C
Jim's Plan to Walk 25 Miles

Walking across America for a sixty-six-year-old man is not a simple task. To walk 3,131 miles in six months was a challenge. It didn't just happen. I had a plan. Daily I worked that plan to make it across America.

My Preparation Before the Walk

1. I created a plan that worked for me. I created it while training and conditioning months before the walk began.
2. I first bought the best shoes as I thought my feet needed the best. Road Runner Sports in Newbury Park fitted me with Brooks Glycerin 10. Perfect. I also was fitted for and bought special pairs of professional inserts. These are a must for long walks.
3. At Road Runner, members of the staff also suggested I rotate shoes during the day. I walked 8-10 miles at a time in one pair of shoes, and then would switch pairs. It kept them fresher. They tend to wear down during the day.
4. Over several months, I gradually built up how many miles a day I could walk.
5. In a trial walk of three successive days to test "recovery" time for my body, I walked 31, 23 and 31 miles and learned a lot. I learned to take breaks and not try to walk a straight 31 miles. It was hard to

recover for the next day. In my training, I learned I could walk 6-8 miles at a time, then rest. To walk 25 miles a day, I could do that by having 3 or 4 walks in an 8-10 hour period.

The Daily Plan during the Walk across America

1. I dressed appropriately daily (see Appendix D—Daily Prep).
2. I planned to walk 25 miles six days a week, resting on Sundays. I averaged a walking pace of about 3.0 mph. Sometimes faster, sometimes slower.
3. I began the day walking 4-6 miles, then took a protein and water break of 15-20 minutes in the RV when Glenda fed me a second breakfast—a hard-boiled egg plus water, coconut water, and electrolyte boost drink. I sat and rested, then walked.
4. I tried to walk at least 6 - 8 more miles before lunch, trying for 12-15 miles before lunch.
5. At lunch I would eat, and then nap for 15-20 minutes after Glenda massaged my feet.
6. After lunch break, I walked 6 more miles before a protein and water break. I rested for a few minutes, then took a Power Bar or Cliff Bar with me to eat as I walked 6 to 7 miles more before dinner and night's rest.
7. During the walk each day, I learned to sit down on a rail or wherever, if tired. A couple of minutes made all the difference in the world for my feet and legs.
8. While walking, I passed the time by eating sunflower or pumpkin seeds (salt), drinking water, praying (talking or chatting with God), waving at trucks and trains, talking to people, memorizing Philippians, enjoying America, dictating into my cassette recorder,

taking pictures with my phone, dreaming, singing, talking to animals, thinking, talking with Glenda and others on the phone when I had reception. It was a full day–every day! Something new and exciting!

Appendix D
Jim's Daily Prep for Walking

1. Wake up. Get out of bed and sit on the "step up" part to our bedroom/bathroom area of RV.
2. Tape my ankles with KT tape when they felt weak or sore.
3. Put on my special walking socks.
4. Put on my elastic ankle brace on each ankle.
5. Put on my long-sleeved Under Armour, then my neon orange shirt, "I'm Walking Across America."
6. Put on my long (and light) walking pants, using sweat pants when it was cooler.
7. Put on "war paint" (sun block) on parts of my skin exposed to the sun. I burn easily.
8. Eat my breakfast, normally cereal with Rice or Almond Milk (allergic to dairy).
9. Put on my glasses and read my daily Bible reading and write in my daily journal.
10. Take my daily vitamin supplements. Take one Aleve if needed.
11. Drink my Pea-Protein mixed in apple juice with L-Glutamine (for muscle recovery).
12. Put on my Garmin watch.
13. Put on my belt that had holders for my cell phone and mini-recorder.

14. In my pants pocket, neon sweatshirt, or light jacket (depending on weather), I would put Blistex, Bluetooth, and two pedometers (one in each pocket). We gauged my mileage using these two pedometers, plus Glenda's iPad and the RV odometer, plus mile markers on the road to arrive at the closest to exact walking miles every day. (Very accurate.)

15. Carried a copied portion of Philippians (Bible book) that I was memorizing.

16. Put on Brooks Glycerin 10 shoes with a shoe number on it. I recorded miles daily for each shoe, often wearing at least two different pair of shoes daily. It helped keep them fresh and lasting longer. I wore out 13 pair of shoes and 3 professional inserts. Put on my broad-brimmed hat.

17. Put on my "inexpensive cloth dermatology gloves" with tips of fingers cut out for me to access things better in my pockets. The gloves helped keep the sun off my hands.

18. Grabbed my walking sticks with a tennis ball on each end to absorb shock when the sticks hid pavement or hard ground. (I wore out over 20 different tennis balls on the *Walk*.)

19. I said to Glenda, "I'm ready. Let's pray." We prayed and either I walked out the door of the RV and started walking (if we parked right where I had stopped walking at night) or Glenda drove me to the exact spot where I had stopped the night before.

20. I was on my way toward my goal of 25 miles for the day. How did I do that every day? I had a plan. (See Appendix C for Jim's Plan to Walk 25 Miles.)